COCKATIEL LESSONS
*how one little yellow bird
changed everything*

by

Marguerite Floyd

Address inquires to
Cracked Seed Publishing
PO Box 11365
Lexington KY 40575
info@crackedseedpublishing.com

ISBN 978-0-9856075-2-4

Acknowledgements

This book would not be possible without a lot of help from a lot of people. In no particular order, I very much appreciated the special efforts of Jessie Franklin, Sue Silverman, Phoebe Linden, Anne Shelby, Bev Harp, Christine Kennedy, Liz Wilson, and of course, Charli, Flash, and Nicholas. Special thanks also to Bianca, Sonia, Virginia, Leah, Donna, Carla, the two Megans, Ronnie, Cathy, and all the other Pennyroyal staff whose names I've forgotten.

The events recounted in this book are based on my experiences and frequently faulty memory. Some names, dates, and events have been changed, and when I forgot specifics I invented as necessary.

Do not depend on the information in this book as medical or behavior advice for your bird. Instead, find yourself a good avian vet and a good parrot behavior consultant.

for Sugar Franklin

Foreword

The hole in the backyard I had had dug three years ago is overgrown now with the season's new grass. Every spring I make a note that I need to have it filled in so no one stumbles over it, and then I promptly forget about it. Just as I have a thousand times before, I remind myself again that I made the right decision.

The wild bird feeder hanging from the tree is empty and I refill it. I prefer the small birds to the grackles and starlings, so I use safflower seed in the feeder. I hang a suet cake just in case any of the larger birds stop by.

I disconnect the cord from the bird bath. It's been a warm March and there will be no more freezing temperatures. All winter the finches and cardinals and mourning doves have eaten their fill in my backyard and splashed happily in the bird bath. Occasionally, the neighbor's cat comes through, drawn by the chirping and singing, but is always surprised to find the birds gone by the time he arrives.

I make a complete circuit around the house, checking that everything has survived the winter intact. As I go back inside the house, I remind myself again to have that hole filled.

Chapter One

I knew I was going to do it, even though I kept telling myself I was just looking.

"Let's just go in and look," I told my mother. I pushed open the door to the pet store. "I want to see their birds."

It was the Saturday before Thanksgiving, 1998, and the store was crowded and noisy with adults in bulky coats and children running to point at the fish tanks or exclaim over the puppies.

Most Valuable Pets was Lexington's newest pet store, already famous for having big colorful parrots on display. I wanted to see if the rumors were true that the parrots were uncaged and allowed to interact with the customers. My mother and I made our way to the back of the store, led by the sounds of squawking and calls.

Most of the birds were on the floor of the big open display while some bigger birds were perched on an artificial tree. Occasionally, a green or red medium-sized bird would venture out of the display's frame and cling to the wall, watching us watching it. There seemed to be all colors and sizes of birds, and their noises drowned out the sounds of humans. Two larger white birds were screeching at each other while a small green one was whistling. I couldn't make out if it was whistling an actual song or just random notes.

"Get one that talks," my mother instructed me. She stood a safe distance away lest any of the birds single her out and poop on her. I was transfixed by the energy and color and noise of the birds; they were all busy preening, fussing at each other, scratching at the bedding, eating, or just walking around. A small gray bird with a tall crest walked over to me and tilted its head up to get a better look.

Lately I'd found myself thinking of having birds in the house again, only maybe one a bit more interactive than the zebra finches I used to have. Finches were shy and really didn't want to be bothered with humans. They were perfectly content to stay in their cage and chirp their little finch chirps. As a child I had had a blue parakeet I named Kim because the word had such an exotic sound, but it had died not long after taking up residence in the living room.

A young man with glasses magically appeared, smiling and ready to be helpful. He had on a headset with the microphone cupped around his face to his mouth.

"I'm thinking about getting a bird," I said. "What kind is this one?" I pointed to the little gray bird, who was now rocking back and forth, like a child waiting for ice cream.

"That's a cockatiel," he said "but he's been sold." He leaned down and scooped up a yellow bird nearby, about the same size and also with a crest. It immediately hopped off his hand and onto my shoulder. Then it ran to the middle of my back.

I froze and then squirmed and twisted and tried to reach the bird with my hands. What if I couldn't grab it? What if I grabbed it and it bit me? A couple of customers turned to watch me. The clerk plucked the bird off my back and placed it on my hand.

It and I looked at each other -- me with a kind of wonder and fear, it with what I imagined was indignation, if birds even felt indignation. It ran to my back again.

Again the clerk put the bird on my hand. I pretended to examine it closely. It was all yellow except for two large round orange spots on its cheeks. Mother pointed out that there was a bald spot on the bird's head, almost hidden by its crest. The clerk assured us that it was a genetic trait of the lutino cockatiel and perfectly normal. "These are great birds," he said. "Everybody loves cockatiels."

I nodded as though I knew what he was talking about. "What do you think," I asked my mother.

"Will it talk?" my mother asked.

"Most of them can," the clerk said cheerfully.

"How old is it?" I asked.

"All these cockatiels are about five months old," he said.

The bird was staying on my finger. It seemed to be studying me, as if it was plotting something. I reminded myself that it was just a bird, incapable of plotting anything.

"Can I pet it?" I asked.

"Sure," the clerk said.

I lifted my free hand and immediately the bird ran up my arm and to the back of my neck and down to the middle of my back. I twisted myself around and bent my arm back, trying to get the bird to come back down my arm. A few more customers turned to watch. My mother had an alarmed look on her face. I felt like an idiot. It was obvious I had no business getting a bird.

The clerk calmly plucked the bird off my back and put it back on my hand.

"What if I get home and it runs to my back again?"

The clerk nodded. "Just take your time. He's used to humans." His headset began crackling and he turned his head and whispered into it.

I looked at my mother. She shrugged. "It's up to you," she said. "You know what you're doing." Of course this was not even remotely true, but my mother always assumes the best of me.

I looked again at the creature on my finger. As if on cue, it immediately ran up my arm and to my back.

"Seriously," I said, "What if I get it home and can't get him off my back?" The way people were staring at us now I began to wonder if the pet store charged a fee for watching idiot customers attempt to pick up birds.

The clerk ended his conversation, plucked the bird off my back, and replaced it on my finger. "You'll get the hang of it," he assured me.

I nodded. "How much?"

"This one is $99."

I took a deep breath and calculated. I could do it. I had recently put myself on a plan to pay off my credit cards, which left me very little extra money, but I could just manage this purchase. I went over in my mind where I had put the finches' old cage and congratulated myself for cleaning it up and storing it, rather than throwing it out.

"All right," I heard myself say.

He nodded and picked up the bird. "I'll get the paperwork."

"Wait," I said. "If I get home and realize I've made an awful mistake can I return it?"

He muttered something about 48 hours. My mother and I watched him vanish into the depths of the store with the bird securely on his hand.

"I was planning to give you $100 for Christmas," mother announced. "Why don't I give it to you now?"

I was surprised but pleased. My mother and I had long since given up on attempting to buy holiday gifts for each other; now we simply traded gift cards or cash and went to nice restaurants for lunch. She was a stylish woman, always impeccably dressed and always looking decades younger than her 70 years. I, on the other hand, was a middle-aged woman happiest in jeans and tee shirts who cared exactly nothing about how young or old I looked.

The clerk returned with a small colorful box with handles from which some scratching sounds could be heard. The box showed a picture of a canary and had the words "I'm going home!" on it. He handed me the box. I was suddenly afraid. I knew nothing about birds other than zebra finches and I hadn't known much about them. I just wanted something alive in my house to keep me company.

"What does he eat?" I asked.

He led me to a counter in the middle of the store. "Our birds are weaned onto Harrison's

8

pellets." He nodded at a row of bags in cream-colored cloth bags.

I picked one up, then glanced at the wall of toys. "Does he need toys?" I was astonished at the colors and sizes and shapes of the wall of toys for birds.

"Yes," he said. I picked the first one I saw, a blue bell-shaped piece of wood with a suede cord. I could see myself coming to this store regularly to buy cloth bags of bird pellets and toys, but I couldn't imagine what it would be like to give the pellets and toys to an actual bird. I was probably making a terrible mistake. I'd never heard of birds playing with toys, but there was a picture of a bird on the toy's label.

My mother and I followed the clerk to the cash register at the front of the store. I lifted the box to my face, but I couldn't see anything through the small holes.

"Now, he may not eat at first," the clerk said. "Give him 24 hours to get used to everything."

"OK," I said. "He won't die, will he?"

The clerk smiled. "No, but if he doesn't eat within 24 hours, give us a call."

Mother and I pooled our money to pay for everything, and I walked her to her car. "Thank you for this," I said. I nodded at the box in my hand.

"You're welcome, honey. I'm glad I could help." She opened her car door. "I'll call you tomorrow."

I watched her drive away, then I got in my car and headed home. I kept glancing at the box.

"Are you okay in there," I asked.

There was a slight scratching sound.

"It'll be okay. We'll be home real soon and I've got a nice big clean cage for you." The scratching stopped for a few moments, then started again.

Oh lord, I thought. What on earth have I done?

Chapter Two

I took a deep breath and opened the box. The yellow bird looked up at me, that odd expression of indignation on its face. I lifted the box and tilted it toward the open door of the cage. I was afraid to attempt to pick the bird up out of the box -- what if it flew out and hid somewhere in the house? There was the sound of scrambling and the bird finally slid into the cage.

It stood very still and looked around slowly. "There are your pellets," I said, pointing to a shallow dish. The pellets were tiny, gray, and hard; I couldn't imagine they tasted very good, but I had to believe the pet store clerk. Maybe birds didn't have taste buds. "And water, in case you're thirsty." I pointed to another shallow dish.

The bird didn't move. We stared at each other. It had red eyes. Its yellow crest feathers were sticking straight up. I'd never really considered the color yellow before, much less on a bird. Yellow was actually a very nice color. The bird's beak was a soft pinkish gray. I wondered if she bit me if it would hurt very much. The clerk had called it a male, but I kept thinking of it as a female. I wanted to touch her, but I was afraid to open the cage door again.

"I hope we can be friends," I said. The bird made no sound and did not move.

"What's your name?"

Silence. I searched its face for some sign of fear but found none of what I imagined cockatiel fear might look like. I had put the cage on a tall plastic storage unit in the living room so that we were eye to eye.

"I'll have to think up a nice name for you." The pet store clerk had told me to let the bird settle in and not fuss over it too much for the first day or so. "Give him a chance to get used to you."

"Tomorrow, then," I said. "We'll come up with a nice name for you tomorrow." I pointed to the pellets again. "You should eat, keep your strength up."

She and I gazed at each for a few more minutes. Finally I went into the kitchen to prepare dinner in order to keep up my strength.

Around nine o'clock, after watching me but otherwise still not moving, the yellow bird yawned, turned her head backwards, and tucked her beak deep into her neck feathers. I found an old beach towel and draped it over the cage. She lifted her head. She flattened her crest to her head and opened her beak at me, but she didn't hiss.

I wondered what she thought of my living room and all the strange new sounds. Or of me. Did she miss her friends at Most Valuable Pets? Had I, perhaps, interrupted her in an important political discussion with another bird? I knew I was being silly because she was just a little bird, but I thought it would be all right to assume she had feelings and curiosity.

The next day was Sunday. As far as I could tell, the yellow bird had not moved at all during the night. The pellets had not been touched. I did see a few spots of greenish gray feces on the newspaper lining the bottom of the cage, so at least she was still alive.

The yellow bird and I faced each other. "How about this," I offered. "I'll name you Sugar because I know you'll be sweet and Franklin because my mom's last name is Franklin." I smiled at the bird. "Well, I guess she'd be your grandmother actually."

Silence.

"Sugar Franklin," I said. I listened to the sound of it, felt how strange it was to say. "Sugar Franklin," I repeated. "How about that for a name?"

Sugar Franklin made no sound and continued to stare at me.

"You should eat. You must be hungry." I took a deep breath and slid the little cage door up enough to put my hand inside.

Sugar Franklin's crest stood straight up and she hissed at me. She took a step back. I touched the bowl of pellets. "You should eat something. They said you were already eating these."

I withdrew my hand, letting the cage door slide closed. Sugar Franklin's crest lowered a little, but she continued to stare at me.

"Don't eat then," I said. "See if I care."

My sarcasm did not seem to bother her. After a few minutes she delicately walked to the bowl of water and dipped her beak in. She lifted her head back to let the water slide down her throat. Again she dipped into the water, again she lifted her head back. I had been used to the finches drinking without having to lift their head. Sugar Franklin's method seemed strange and exotic. She walked away from the water bowl and resumed watching me. She tilted her head a little to the side as if she had heard something amazing. I thought it was the most adorable thing I'd seen in years.

By late afternoon she still had not touched the pellets. I called the pet store and asked to speak to the clerk who had sold the bird to me. "It's been almost 24 hours," I said. "She hasn't eaten a thing. What should I do?"

"Give her some more time. She'll be okay. If she still isn't eating tomorrow, call us back."

I reluctantly agreed and put the phone down.

"If I let you out," I said to her, "will you promise not to run to my back where I can't reach you?"

She stared at me.

Slowly I opened the cage door and stuck my index finger at her. She backed up and hissed. I didn't move. After some consideration, she delicately climbed onto my index finger.

I held my breath and slowly withdrew my bird-laden finger from the cage.

Sugar Franklin immediately ran up my wrist, up my arm, and to the back of my neck.

Panic swelled into my stomach. I put my hand behind my back and with a lot of twisting managed to chase Sugar Franklin back to my shoulder. I turned my head to her. "I'm going to pet you now," I said. I lifted my hand, and Sugar quickly moved to my back again.

Once I managed to get her back to my shoulder again, I decided to put her back in her cage. If I could. She refused to step onto my hand, so I finally opened the cage door, squatted down, and leaned my shoulder against the cage. "Go on," I urged. She refused to move. "Go on, Sugar Franklin." The name still sounded strange.

What was I going to do if she wouldn't go into the cage? What if she flew off? How could I catch her? What had possessed me to buy a bird in the first place? Was I now officially insane? Was this going to be the only way to get her in or out of the cage? I was a 45-year-old presumably adult, educated woman -- why hadn't I gotten a dog or a cat, like normal adult people do?

I nudged my shoulder against the opening in the cage, with no response from Sugar Franklin. I straightened back up. Trying again, I held my index finger up to her. She politely stepped onto my finger as if she'd been patiently waiting for the opportunity the entire time. Her weight felt substantial but not so heavy that she would tire out my finger. I was glad she was just a bird and unable to read my thoughts or know how inexperienced I was.

I gently placed her inside the cage and closed the door. She looked around for a moment, then walked to the water bowl and drank. Her steps were clumsy, and I wondered if perhaps she was crippled or brain-damaged. Weren't birds supposed to be graceful? What if the pet store had sold me a defective bird?

After she had drunk her fill, she calmly walked (stumbling once) to the dish of pellets, looked them over, and then began to eat.

I offered up a silent prayer of thanks. She was eating! She wasn't going to starve to death.

"Tomorrow I'll take you on a tour of the house," I told her.

My mother called, and I assured her that all was well with the new bird. No, I said, she wasn't talking yet. It was probably a little too early to expect that.

All that afternoon I did research on the Internet. I learned that cockatiels were parrots just like the big colorful birds that lived in the rain forests, that they were the second most popular pet bird, and that cockatiels could be expected to live seven to eleven years.

Most surprising to me was that cockatiels (and all parrots) should be eating vegetables but not too many seeds. I thought all birds loved seeds. In fact, I had been planning to buy some for Sugar, in addition to her pellets. I learned that parrots should not eat or drink chocolate, alcohol, caffeine, or avocado. I learned that the fumes from an overheated non-stick cooking pan would kill a parrot.

No chocolate or guacamole? Surely no one would expect me to get rid of all my non-stick pans, would they? Things seemed to be getting a lot more complicated than I had counted on.

But at least now she was eating.

Chapter Three

Before I left for work on Monday, I refilled Sugar's pellets and water. As far as I could tell she was pooping on a regular basis, and it seemed to look all right though I wasn't exactly sure what cockatiel poop was supposed to look like. I had always left the radio on for the finches while I was at work, so I turned it on and hoped it would help her not be too bored during the day. The toy I had bought for her hung in the cage, untouched.

At the time I had an answering machine that allowed me to monitor sounds in the house. About ten o'clock I called my number, pressed the right numbers, and listened. I heard the very faint sound of the radio, but nothing else. I hung up and called back so I could leave a message that Sugar could hear.

"Hi Sugar Franklin," I said into the receiver. "Are you doing okay? I'll be home soon." I tried to imagine her hearing my voice over the sounds of the radio. I hoped the phone hadn't startled her. Was she tilting her head a little to the side in that way I found so cute?

I hung up, feeling like an idiot and grateful for having a private office.

That afternoon I rushed home, and as soon as I put the key in the door I heard loud chirps. There she was, walking back and forth, back and forth, so quickly she was nearly a blur. She was glad to see me, I thought. It was a miracle.

I looked into the cage and said hello. She stopped pacing, placed herself at the door of the cage, and looked up at me. She chirped.

"I missed you, too," I said. "Let me change clothes first." Her chirps followed me into the bedroom as I changed clothes. I felt as excited as she seemed to be.

I gathered up all my courage and let the little yellow bird step onto my finger. We walked down the hall to the study. I sat down at my desk, let Sugar Franklin climb onto my shoulder, and powered up the Macintosh. Sugar examined everything intently, actually seeming to listen to me explain things.

"This is where I spend a lot of time," I told her.

She graciously stepped onto my finger when I held it up to her, and I let her step off onto the desk. She stumbled just a bit, and I wondered again at her awkwardness. My desk was the usual mess of papers and books, so maybe she had just tripped on a pencil or something. She stood still for a long time, surveying everything around her. Her tail feathers were dirty on the ends as if she'd been dragging herself through dirt. Two of them were broken and hanging at angles.

She climbed onto a splayed-open paperback so she could get a better view of my hands on the keyboard. She watched me type "cockatiel" into Google. I soon found a discussion board called "Tiel Talk." I read through some of the postings and felt reassured that the members seemed to know what they were talking about.

Keeping an eye on Sugar Franklin, who was still standing motionless, I typed in a message. "I just got a cockatiel. She's five months old. Is that an adult or still a baby?" I pressed the Enter key and waited.

While I waited, hoping someone would respond quickly, I offered my finger to the bird. She delicately stepped up, then ran up my shoulder.

A few minutes later I received a response from one of the moderators. "Five months is still very much a baby. You'll find a lot of helpful people here, so don't be afraid to ask questions."

A baby? Sugar looked at me. I offered her my finger, but she hissed and backed away.

"She stumbles a lot," I wrote. "Is this normal or does she have brain damage? And she has two broken tail feathers."

"Perfectly normal for a baby," someone else wrote back. "It can take a while for them to figure everything out and how to hold their feathers."

I thanked whoever it was who had written me and wondered how many cockatiels she had that she knew so much about babies. I found it astonishing that a bird had to learn what it was about. I had always thought birds knew everything they needed to know as soon as they left the nest. It would never have occurred to me that a bird had to learn how to hold her feathers up. Were there other things she would have to learn to do? Who would teach her those things? I had a hard enough time being a human; I couldn't think of anything I could teach a little bird.

I logged off, and offered my finger to Sugar again. She stepped up and then ran to the back of my neck.

"I am not going to hurt you," I told her. "If you'd let me pet you, you'd see that. I bet you'd love to be petted, wouldn't you?"

The bird did not move until I went back to the living room. She stepped up onto my finger and reluctantly went into her cage. I closed the cage door, and she began running back and forth, back and forth, wanting out. When it was clear I was not going to let her out again, she stopped pacing and glared at me.

I refilled the food and water dishes and changed the papers. She climbed to the top of the perch in order to watch. I had the feeling she was supervising me, rating how well I did my chores. What was she going to do, write me up on some avian evaluation form? I hadn't been prepared for a creature that had such personality. I thought birds were . . . well, just birds.

I had the same results with Sugar Franklin on Tuesday and Wednesday and Thursday nights. Sometimes I let her stay out on top of her cage or took her into the study with me until bedtime, but no matter how sweetly I talked to her she wouldn't allow me to pet her. I was beginning to think it was always going to be this way. On Friday I'd had another bad day at work, and I drove home depressed and disheartened.

From the outside it seemed I had a wonderful job. I had been hired as a documentation manager for the university hospital to oversee and coordinate policies and other important publications, but because of endless reorganizations I had somehow ended up in a department that gathered data for insurance and accreditation purposes.

That Friday I had learned my manager had volunteered me for yet another assignment over a month ago but, as usual, had not bothered mentioning it to me. The assignment required a lot of data crunching, even though I had repeatedly explained to him my inability to do that type of work. Beyond basic addition and subtraction I was hopeless with numbers, and I would never have applied for any job that required data analysis. I couldn't even fully understand what the project was about.

Two administrators had refused to sign hospital policies that day because they never signed anything lest they obligate themselves or their departments, which left me to explain to the hospital director why the policies were late and unsigned.

I was continually applying for transfers within the university system, but the automated job matching system seemed designed to cull out candidates rather than match them with open jobs. That day I had learned that a job I had applied and interviewed for had been given to the niece of an administrator from the athletics department.

I enjoyed most of the people I worked with, but more than 15 years there had worn me out. I was no longer shocked to hear top-level administrators screaming at employees and calling them names, or hearing about two-digit percentage raises for certain employees while the rest of us were told there was no money for raises, or having to make do with overcrowded offices with crumbling ceiling tiles and leaking pipes while the wing of administrative offices was remodeled every two years.

I didn't have the heart to move out of state; what close family members I had left were here and almost all my friends lived here. I felt far too old to pick up and start over in a strange place. It didn't help that I was independent and outspoken in a world where there was no room for anyone who didn't exactly fit the mold. I was just as surely caught as an animal in a trap.

When I got home I opened Sugar's cage, and she stepped onto my hand and ran to the back of my neck. I sat there, wishing for the millionth time I could find a way out but knowing it was hopeless. And now I had this bird who wanted nothing to do with me. Yeah, I'd arranged a fine mess for myself, I thought.

I felt Sugar Franklin slowly inch her way to my shoulder. Then I felt her warm and soft head press against the side of my neck.

I froze. She pushed her head against my neck again, more insistently this time. I turned to look at her and saw her looking at me expectantly. I raised my hand and tentatively touched her. She lowered her head and allowed me to stroke her crest.

I offered her my hand and she stepped onto it with no fuss. I lowered her to my chest and began to pet her slowly and gently. It was magic -- this soft, warm little yellow creature finally trusting me enough to allow me to pet her. My eyes filled with tears. She moved her head a little to the side so I would pet her around her ear, then moved her head a little to the other side lest I miss the other ear. She was completely absorbed by the petting.

"Thank you," I whispered. "How did you know I was feeling bad?" Sugar Franklin made no answer.

As I petted her I saw that her feathers were not all yellow. Some of the feathers on her wings were actually cream-colored but so small they blended into the yellow ones. Her orange cheeks were actually short orange feathers that I imagined were a tiny bit stiffer to the touch than the rest of her feathers. I was astonished to see that she even had little eyelashes (later I learned they were actually tiny bristly feathers).

She didn't like me to touch her wings; when I did, she snapped at me. If I petted her head the wrong way, she would snap at me. These weren't bites but more of a reprimand that I wasn't doing things correctly. I apologized each time before I tried to pet another spot. She most especially liked it when I stroked her head feathers backward; this was what parrot owners called "scritching." She would allow scritching for hours or whenever my fingers gave out.

Her toes and nails were pink, now that she allowed me close. Her beak was light. Every inch of her was astonishingly beautiful.

We soon created a pattern to the days. I would cover her cage when I was ready for bed, usually around 10 or 11. In the mornings I would uncover the cage, tell her to have a good day, turn on the television for her, then go to work. Sometimes I would call and listen in, sometimes I would talk to her via the answering machine.

When I got home she would run back and forth, back and forth, in her cage, until I let her out. She would hop onto my shoulder and supervise me for the rest of the evening, chirping helpfully in my ear if she saw something interesting, such as clothes being put into the washer, or nipping me if I didn't do something to her satisfaction, such as petting her whenever she wanted.

One lazy afternoon I was in the study with Sugar Franklin. I had part of a small can of peanuts, and I spent over an hour handing her tiny bits. She would daintily take one of the bits from my hand, eat it, and wait for me to deliver the next one. Which I did until the can was almost empty.

I was fascinated at how she would lift her foot to scratch her ear; her toes going so fast they were a blur, her little eyes closed to better concentrate. The natural curve of her closed beak gave the appearance of a little smile when I petted her. Whenever she yawned, I could glimpse her tiny tongue curling in her mouth. In the evenings she rubbed her upper beak against the lower one, making a soft rasping sound I found oddly soothing. My growing number of Internet friends with parrots told me it was the sound parrots made when they were relaxed and happy.

I read somewhere that parrots invented tai chi. I believed it. Sugar would balance on her right leg and slowly, indolently stretch her left leg and wing behind her at the same time. She would lower her left leg and wing, then repeat the motion with her right leg and wing. Then she would shake herself out, fluffing out her feathers and causing dander and tiny wisps of down feathers to float out in the air.

I began to refer to her as the little yellow bird as frequently as I called her Sugar Franklin.

I gathered up my old non-stick skillet and a couple of pans with non-stick surfaces and gave them to Goodwill. My mother, who had also heard that non-stick was deadly to birds, brought me a couple of well-seasoned cast iron skillets.

My mother lived 70 miles away but called frequently. I had been raised by my grandmother because of bitter battles between my parents. Now that my grandmother and father were dead, my mother and I spent more time together, getting to know one another again. I tried to explain my growing fascination with Sugar, but she couldn't see the attraction. As far as she was concerned all animals belonged outside.

"Is she talking yet?" she would ask. When I said no, she would say that maybe Sugar would get the hang of talking soon. I could tell her philosophy was that there wasn't any point in having a bird if it wouldn't talk.

Actually I wasn't too worried about Sugar Franklin never talking. I talked to her like one person talking to another, and she would indicate by her body language if she was listening or not. When she was paying attention she would study me with one eye and then the other or just stand still and stare at me.

There was no question in my mind that Sugar Franklin understood me. She was especially familiar with the word "no" and what it meant. Not that she ever paid any attention to it. Most of the time she ignored anything I said; she would turn her back to me or continue doing whatever it was I wanted her to stop doing, such as trying to chew up the telephone cord, until I pulled her away, fussing and hissing.

One afternoon Sugar Franklin was playing in her usual spot on the desk beside me in the office. She was chewing an old plastic key chain I'd given her. After a few minutes I heard it fall to the floor. I picked it up and put it back on the desk without paying much attention. Again it fell to the floor, and again I picked it up and put it back on the desk, a little further from the edge this time. Barely a minute passed before the key chain fell again. I picked it up and put it back, then watched as Sugar picked it up with her beak, walked to the edge of the desk, and dropped it on the floor. She tilted her head to eye it on the floor then looked at me expectantly.

I learned later this was called the "I'll Drop It and You Pick It Up" game, and that many parrots instigate it with their humans. If it was a test I evidently had passed because I was always willing to pick up the items she dropped.

Another evening when I took her into the office with me, I let her play on the left side of my Mac where I'd put some nice pieces of scrap paper for her to chew. I removed the cap from a bottle of water and tossed it onto the pile of papers in front of Sugar, thinking she might like to chew it as well.

I was engrossed in reading about parrots on the Internet and was vaguely aware of Sugar scooting the bottle cap around the desk. I glanced over to see her pick up the cap in her beak and drop it on the papers again; I wanted to be ready if she was starting a new round of "I'll Drop It and You Pick It Up." She chirped at me when I turned my attention back to the Mac. She chirped several more times, but not hearing anything fall to the floor I remained focused on the screen. A few seconds later the water bottle cap came skidding across the keyboard. I jerked back and looked at her. She was standing there with a disgusted expression on her face, looking me directly in the eye. I expected her to start stomping her little feet.

"Oh!" I said. "Are you thirsty?" I poured some water into the bottle cap and offered it to her. She delicately took several sips, tipping her head back after each one to let the water flow down her throat. When she had finished she gave me a withering, dismissive look, turned her back to me, and began chewing on a pencil.

I watched her for a few minutes, realizing that she was far more clever than any of my finches. She was so smart, in fact, that I probably needed to read up more on cockatiels. Suddenly abstract Internet information about parrots wasn't as intriguing as Sugar Franklin.

The next day I stopped at the bookstore for some books about cockatiels. The most current ones were *Guide to a Well-Behaved Parrot* by Mattie Sue Athan and *The Pleasure of Their Company* by Bonnie Munro Doane.

Both authors said that parrots need to be taught the rules of the house and how to behave themselves, which made perfect sense to me. The first thing I needed to do, they wrote, was teach Sugar Franklin how to "step up."

This puzzled me because Sugar almost always stepped onto my finger when I offered it, but I took the experts seriously. Over the next weeks I would hold out my hand, thumb tucked behind my palm, and gently press the top of her legs and say, "Step up!" She always stepped onto my finger with an air of a queen stepping up to the podium to address her subjects. I taught her to step up onto a pencil and then a dowel rod. She was smart, all right. The few times she didn't want to step up, I persisted and she obeyed, but then she would attempt to bite me for bothering her.

I would praise her whenever she did as I asked; both books emphasized the importance of positive reinforcement, though I didn't realize that was what I was doing. I said "Good bird!" a million times, and she would fluff up and shake out her feathers, a gesture I finally decided was a sign of pleasure.

It became so habitual that I frequently caught myself saying, "Good bird!" to my mother when she told me interesting news.

She would feign indignation and say, "I am not your bird," and we would both laugh.

Parrots were flock animals, I read. They did everything together because it was safer that way. I began to notice that whenever I brought my dinner into the living room, Sugar Franklin would watch and wait until I began to eat before digging into her own food dish. If she heard a strange noise in the house, she would pull her feathers tight against her body, making herself skinny, and look at me for a sign if she should continue to be alert or could safely ignore the sound. When I decided to take a nap on the couch beside her cage, she too would tuck her head into her neck feathers and sleep.

I had read that some people potty trained their parrots, so that was my next project. Being a small bird, Sugar Franklin's poops were small but frequent. One evening I estimated that she pooped about once every 15 minutes or so. After one of her poops, I moved the wastepaper basket in front of me and then waited. About 12 minutes later I had her step up, and I held her over the wastepaper basket.

She kept trying to climb up my arm, but I insisted she stay on my finger over the wastepaper basket. "Poop!" I said cheerfully. The books said to have a cue word, so I said it with a lot of excitement.

She stood on my finger, wondering what I was doing.

"Go poop!" I said.

She started to climb up my arm again, but I shifted my arm so she had to stay on my finger.

"Poop! Time to poop!"

The look she gave me was a mixture of confusion and disgust. It was always surprising to me how much expression her face showed -- a creature with a beak can't smile or frown, and with no eyebrows or lips or facial muscles to indicate a mood. Yet I almost always knew what she was feeling just by looking at her little face and body language and how she held her feathers.

Fifteen minutes came and went, with no poop.

"Poop!" I said. "You probably need to *poop* now. Just go ahead and *poop* right into the wastepaper basket."

She stood on my finger and looked at me.

At the twenty-minute mark my arm was tired so I gave up and put her back on the coffee table. Where she immediately pooped then sauntered off to chew on a magazine.

I wiped up the tiny spot of poop with a tissue and considered trying again in fifteen minutes, but then decided against it. Her poops were so small it probably wasn't worth all the trouble.

That weekend I was attempting to balance my checkbook late one evening. I was sitting on the couch with my feet on the coffee table while Sugar Franklin was busily chewing up some paper. The coffee table was littered with pens and books and to-do lists, a small bottle of aspirin, and what not. At one point she decided to climb up my legs and onto the couch. She walked to the end of the couch and prepared to climb onto my stereo receiver. I had covered the receiver with a dishcloth to guard against accidental poops because she liked to stand on top of it.

I leaned over and picked her up. "You know you're not allowed up there," I told her. I put her back on the coffee table and returned to my calculations.

She immediately climbed up on my legs again and went directly to the receiver. I told her no, picked her up, and put her back on the coffee table. She chirped angrily at me, climbed back up my legs again, and hurried to the receiver.

I picked her up without comment and put her back on the coffee table.

A few seconds later she repeated her trip. "I said no," I said, picking her up and depositing her on the coffee table yet again. I went back to my figuring.

I heard something fall to the floor in front of me. I looked up just in time to see Sugar using her beak to push the aspirin bottle to the floor. As I watched she pushed one of the pens off the coffee table, followed by a small pad of paper and then a paper clip.

Sugar Franklin gave me a withering look and turned her back to me. I finally closed my mouth and made myself keep a straight face. I picked her up and, without ceremony or comment, put her in her cage. She immediately went to her sleeping perch, tucked her head in her neck feathers, and fell asleep.

I draped the towel over her cage. As I picked everything up and rearranged things on the coffee table I knew I was going to need a lot more than two books.

Chapter Four

I found dozens of Internet bulletin boards and web pages and discussion groups devoted to parrots. There were even such people as parrot "behaviorists," which I immediately assumed were frauds preying on ignorant parrot owners. Yet, as I researched further it seemed that many of these "behaviorists" were the same people writing articles that made the most sense to me: Liz Wilson, Phoebe Linden, Mattie Sue Athan, Kashmir Csaky.

I learned that there are hundreds of species of parrots; many of them endangered. Only cockatiels and parakeets were said to be domesticated; otherwise, all parrots are still considered wild, as if brought into our homes directly from the rain forest.

Sugar Franklin was a "mutation;" that is, she had been bred to have that beautiful yellow color called "lutino." The natural colors of a cockatiel are gray and white with yellow faces and orange cheeks. How the mutation had been done was beyond me; charts and tables of mating this type of cockatiel with that type of cockatiel were too complex and bewildering. It didn't matter anyway; Sugar Franklin was beautiful no matter how it had been arranged.

As the months went on Sugar became more fascinating as well as familiar. I began sending frequent e-mail reports to friends at work and from college, never imagining anyone could find such information boring. None of them had parrots so they shared my continual surprise at the things I was learning.

My friends considered me to be an intelligent and independent person, but they also knew I was frequently obsessed with new ideas and odd projects. When I was working toward my master of fine arts in writing, I would send them poems I thought appropriate as well as interesting gossip about teachers and other students. Everyone assumed Sugar Franklin was just one more of my special interests.

Sugar Franklin developed an odd obsession with my toes, both with and without socks. Whenever she saw them she would tighten her feathers, lower her crest, and hiss at them. My toes angered her so much I worried she would attack them, but she never went further than the threatening posture and hissing. Some cockatiels serenaded their humans' toes, but Sugar Franklin found nothing in my toes worth singing about. I spent some extra time studying my toes but couldn't find anything objectionable about them.

Other people had cockatiels that talked and sang and whistled, so I decided I would teach Sugar Franklin to whistle. I began whistling *You Are My Sunshine* and the Andy Griffith song to her countless times a day. She would cock her head and listen intently for a few seconds, then ignore me. No matter how often I whistled, she refused to even try.

Some afternoons I would take her into the study with me, where she would find pencils and start chewing on them. I would glance over and there she would be, her beak, tongue, and mouth black with graphite as if that were the most normal thing in the world.

I had never wanted children, but I suspected a small parrot could be as worrisome as a two-year-old human. Maybe more so.

The experts I found on the Internet kept talking about avian veterinarians. I'd been raised by people who considered animals as workers or food and little else. Any pet I had that got sick was expected to get well on its own or die; we couldn't waste good money on long, drawn-out expensive vet care.

But what if Sugar Franklin had an accident? Or flew out of the house by accident and got injured? I could not bear to think of her hurt, so I decided I should have at least a record on file with one of these special vets in case there was ever an emergency. I just wouldn't get caught up in a lot of unnecessary "routine" expensive care she didn't need.

I asked friends if there was a local veterinarian who specialized in birds.

"Pennyroyal," was the immediate and universal answer. "Dr. Bianca Zaffarano." There was another avian vet named Virginia Garrison in town, but she was rumored to have retired.

Pennyroyal Small & Exotic Animal Hospital turned out to be a small building that looked like all of the houses in the neighborhood. A set of railroad tracks ran behind the clinic, and a small bright flag of a colorful parrot beside the door flapped in the wind. Pictures of parrots hung on the walls. A huge silver cat lay sprawled out on the receptionist's desk, ignoring me while I filled out the paperwork.

Dr. Bianca Zaffarano was a tall beautiful woman with dark hair and a large smile. I explained I just wanted a record on file for Sugar in case she ever needed emergency care. Dr. Zaffarano told me everyone called her Dr. Z and then explained the well-bird exam to me, which sounded exactly like what I had read about on the Web.

She gently took Sugar Franklin out of the box the pet store had given me. Sugar immediately began squawking and trying to get loose. Dr. Z did a thorough exam, noting that Sugar was most likely a female because of the markings on her tail feathers. I couldn't distinguish any of the markings or "bars" she pointed out, but I took her word for it. She explained that Sugar would lose all the barred feathers during her first molt and they would be replaced with her adult feathers, which wouldn't have the same markings.

She dipped a cotton-tipped swab into a small fresh poop Sugar dropped on the counter and smeared it on a slide. They would do a "gram stain" on the specimen to look for parasites and diseases.

Sugar Franklin screamed and fought and struggled as if her wings were being sawed off with a dull dinner knife, yet I could see that Dr. Z was being very gentle. I was impressed at how well she could hold the struggling creature with just two fingers around the neck and the bird's back resting in her palm.

"I know you aren't hurting her," I said, "so why is she making such a fuss?"

She smiled. "Oh, cockatiels have to be dramatic about everything."

This pleased me for some reason, as though having a diva parrot were a sign of honor. I smiled, too.

Dr. Z and I discussed cutting Sugar Franklin's wing feathers. "A good trim," she told me, "will allow her to fly but not gain altitude." I considered the possibility of a cat or dog trying to attack Sugar Franklin; she would be able to get away, I imagined, but not fly away from me. I agreed after Dr. Z assured me it wouldn't hurt Sugar Franklin at all.

She deftly clipped a small piece from a few of Sugar's wing feathers and then put her on the counter. Sugar Franklin immediately flew off the counter and across the room, but glided gently to the floor. Just as Dr. Z had said, Sugar could still fly but just not gain altitude.

Dr. Z took a small bit of blood from Sugar's neck, and kept her fingers pressed against the site for a long time in case the blood didn't clot quickly. She handed me a packet of information about pet birds, still holding Sugar, and said the pet store where I had found Sugar was a good one. She talked about how many sick birds she saw from other pet stores in the area but was careful not to mention any store names.

She opened a cabinet and asked if Sugar Franklin liked Nutriberries.

"I've never heard of them," I said.

She checked again that Sugar Franklin was not bleeding from the blood draw and released the squirming mass of feathers onto the counter.

She opened up a small plastic container and offered Sugar a small round ball of what looked like seeds stuck together.

Sugar Franklin immediately leaned over and began eating it, allowing most of it to fall out of her beak, the way she did with everything she ate.

"Okay," I said, knowing the strange looking treats would become a necessity in my house. "Where do I get these things? And what are they called again?"

Dr. Z laughed and wrote down the name. "Most birds love them."

She said the lab results would be available in a few days and might contradict her, but she thought that Sugar Franklin was a healthy normal cockatiel.

She looked inside the box I'd used to bring in Sugar. There was some poop on the bottom of it. Dr. Z briskly tore off a length of paper towel and placed it in the bottom of the box. I felt embarrassed I hadn't thought of that, as if it was perfectly all right to let Sugar Franklin walk in her own feces. I very much did not want this person to think badly of me or view me as a person who didn't take care of her bird. I would be more careful and diligent the next time. In fact, I decided I would get a small cage just for the purpose of traveling.

After we got home and I got Sugar Franklin settled in her cage, I went to the pet store. They had a bewildering array of Nutriberries -- vegetable, fruit, hot pepper, tropical. I didn't know what kind Dr. Z had given her, and at $6 for a small bag I didn't want to get something Sugar wouldn't like. I stopped a clerk, who said that parrots tended to like all of the

varieties so I would be safe with any of them. I
bought the vegetable kind.

There was, as the clerk had said, no reason
for me to worry. Sugar Franklin ate Nutriberries like
she was starving. The little balls were almost as big
as her head. She would hunker down and attack
them with her beak, take a few of the seeds in her
mouth, chew, and let the rest fall to the bottom of
the cage. The instructions on the bag implied it was
all right to let her eat all she wanted. Besides, if Dr. Z
herself gave them to birds they must be all right.

Friday morning Pennyroyal called with the
results of the blood work. Sugar Franklin's results
showed signs of yeast. I had no idea what that meant
but I assumed it was bad. I hurried to the clinic to
pick up a powder that I was to put in her drinking
water to clear it up. She also had some sort of
elevated levels of something related to her liver. Dr.
Z recommended I begin feeding her Roudybush
Liver Crumbles, which I also picked up at
Pennyroyal.

As the weekend progressed I noticed that
Sugar seemed more and more tired. She sat on the
bottom of the cage, sleepy. She refused to eat her
Harrison pellets and even Nutriberries and Liver
Crumbles didn't tempt her. Clearly she was sick, but
I didn't know what to do. I was afraid if I called
Pennyroyal they would charge me hundreds of
dollars for an emergency visit, and I simply didn't
have the money. I would just have to wait until
Monday and hope for the best.

When Monday morning came I was at
Pennyroyal by 7:30, without calling ahead or making

an appointment. Dr. Z called me into the exam room and I related how I'd been giving her the prescribed medication in water, how long it was before Sugar began showing signs of fatigue and not eating. Dr. Z shook her head and said I'd have to give her a different medication, by syringe this time.

She prepared a syringe, held onto Sugar, and demonstrated how I was to stick the syringe in Sugar's beak and press the plunger. I was horrified and terrified. What little I knew of bird anatomy made me aware that there were two "tubes," next to one another -- one for food and one for air. If I injected the medication into the wrong tube I'd drown her.

With trembling fingers I tried to hold Sugar with one hand and lifted the now-empty syringe with the other hand. Sugar Franklin immediately began screaming and struggling until she got loose and flew across the room. Dr. Z picked her up and held her while I tried again. With even less success than the first time.

I would have to do this once a day for a week.

The next day Sugar Franklin was preening on top of her cage. I prepared the syringe and she stopped to watch me warily. As I approached her she opened her beak and hissed at me.

"I'm sorry," I said, "but you're sick and we have to do this." Somehow I managed to hold her head still and get the syringe into her mouth. Was I supposed to point the syringe to the left? Or to the right? Was it my right? Or her left? Which one was it? I was so afraid I had already forgotten what Dr. Z had told me. How far back was I supposed to push the syringe, or was I supposed to just barely stick it inside her beak? Fifty-fifty shot, I told myself. I squeezed my eyes shut, whispered a tiny prayer, and slowly pushed the plunger. I pulled the syringe out of her mouth and looked at her.

She froze, with her beak slightly open. For several long seconds she didn't move, didn't even breathe.

Oh my god, I thought. A sick feeling filled my stomach. I've killed her. I've barely had her long enough to bond with her and now I've killed her.

Finally, she gasped with a thick wet sound. She wheezed and continued to stand stock still.

"Come on, baby," I whispered. "Come on."

She had an expression of shock on her face and it seemed to take forever for her to breathe again. A horrible wheezing sound. I dared not touch her or even allow myself to move.

She wheezed again and slowly looked around. She looked back at me, with what seemed to be bewilderment, her beak still open.

After what felt like several hours but was probably another few seconds, Sugar Franklin leaned down and wiped her beak on the towel covering her cage. She lifted her head and looked at me again. I offered her my finger and she stepped up.

I slowly and gently moved her to the inside of her cage. She delicately stepped onto her favorite perch, where she sat for a few minutes. Then she climbed down and trotted over to her food dish and pecked at one of the Nutriberries.

I sagged with relief. I had not killed her. I washed the syringe and put it away with the tiny bottle of medicine. I was not going to do this again. If I had to take her into the clinic every day and let Dr. Z do it, fine, I'd just have to find the money somehow. I would not put Sugar or myself through that again.

One of the staff from Pennyroyal called the next afternoon to check on her. "She's eating like a hog," I said. And, in fact, she seemed to have regained her appetite, especially for Nutriberries.

Sugar Franklin quickly returned to her normal self, without any further medication. I never told Dr. Z I hadn't given her all of the medicine, and I was pretty confident Sugar wouldn't tell either.

Chapter Five

Sugar Franklin loved to travel in the car, and I
sometimes took her with me to visit my mother or
out-of-state friends. She would chirp happily at the
scenery going past the window. Other times I took
her with me to fast-food drive-throughs, and then
give her bits of french fries through the bars of her
travel cage.

As a flock animal she always seemed to want
to eat whatever I was eating. I began offering her
tiny bits of different foods. She liked grapes, carrots,
apples, corn, eggs, and popcorn, but dismissed any
other vegetables or fruits. She enjoyed Cheerio's and
warm oatmeal and cooked pasta, which she happily
smeared all over her beak. She even liked cooked
chicken, which I thought was strange but my reading
confirmed a lot of cockatiels liked chicken and that it
was all right for her to have it. In addition to
Nutriberries she loved millet seed, which I bought in
big stalks that I clipped to the side of her cage.

Many cockatiels enjoy various lettuces, but
every time I offered lettuce, Sugar would roll around
in the leaves as if the bowl was filled with warm
scented bath water and she was Cleopatra. She
didn't like to bathe in a shallow bowl of water and
she barely tolerated spray baths, but she showed
great enthusiasm for wet or even barely damp
lettuce.

I had an old halogen lamp attached to the
wall over the sofa. Whenever Sugar had a bath, or at
least a good roll in some lettuce, she would climb to
the top of the sofa and preen herself under the

warmth of the lamp. The tiny bits of down she released would float through the rays of light from the lamp.

Sugar Franklin's first molt had been a shock. She wasn't yet a year old when I came home from work one day to find yellow feathers and white down feathers all over the floor and her cage. There were so many I wondered how she could have any left on her body. As I stood there and watched, a feather floated off of her wing.

"You poor baby!" I said. I took her out of the cage and tried to pet her, but she was cranky and didn't want to be touched. I couldn't blame her. A bird has thousands of feathers that naturally renew themselves by new ones pushing out old ones. The new feather shafts are covered in keratin and are exquisitely sensitive as the feather grows to its full length. Sugar Franklin demanded petting all the time to relieve her itchy skin and then nipped me for touching the new feathers. I gave her more frequent spray baths during this time, which seemed to help a little, though she wasn't crazy about bathing.

Several books and articles I read mentioned that malnutrition was still the cause of most pet parrot deaths because so many people still believed that birds lived on seed alone. Unwittingly, people bought bags of seed that were old or even spoiled. Birds generally love seed, but a diet of seed alone is like a human eating nothing but chocolate. Tasty but eventually deadly.

On Tiel Talk many members shared recipes for birdie bread, so naturally it wasn't long before I was making my own versions. Birdie bread is usually based on cornbread mixed with seeds, eggs, mashed vegetables, and/or baby foods, and then baked. The seeds and bread disguised the vegetables, so that Sugar took in more necessary nutrients.

My friends and co-workers continued to listen patiently to me chatter on and on about Sugar Franklin and parrot nutrition and road trips and molting. I probably sounded worse than a first-time mother with her newborn, but I didn't care. Any new behavior sparked a new search for more information. A random post on a parrot discussion board would send me off for hours of more research.

Sugar's cage cart was stuffed with toys and gadgets, even a flight suit I couldn't get her to wear. Parrot-related items and snacks and treats cluttered up the coffee table and end tables. I was always on the outlook for that one special thing that Sugar would fall in love with. Between expensive pellets in cloth-covered bags, new toys, Nutriberries, and books about parrots I soon had no disposable income. I resigned myself to being poor. As long as Sugar Franklin was happy, I was happy.

There were many times I went out in public and discovered I had bird poop on my shoulder or down the back of my tee-shirt. These occurrences didn't bother me nearly as much as I suspected they should. Besides, I read on Tiel Talk that it happened to everyone.

I loved reading about the hundreds of species of parrots, each one more exciting to learn about than the last. I knew it wouldn't be long before I would have to have another parrot. Or two. Sugar

Franklin was wonderful, but what would it be like to live with an entirely different, bigger parrot? It would be so wonderful if I had another parrot and he became friends with Sugar Franklin. Maybe even one that talked? Certainly that would make my mother happy.

I tried to be sensible in my search, and I discussed the options with Sugar Franklin, though she didn't seem interested. I knew I wouldn't be able to tolerate the normal loud squawks of a macaw or cockatoo, but there were so many other species of parrots: conures, Amazons, poicephalus, love birds, eclectus, African greys. There were also the various subspecies, and all with different personalities.

Now that I had learned to recognize a macaw from an Amazon from a pionus I enjoyed visiting the different species at Most Valuable Pets. It was also good therapy when things were bad at work. One afternoon I spied an interesting looking middle-sized parrot with a gray head and a reddish chest. He stepped onto my finger without hesitation. He was twice as big as Sugar Franklin but his weight felt fine in my hand. The bird began to climb up my arm.

"No," I said, remembering all the warnings I'd read about letting birds on shoulders. I gently moved him to my other hand, where he gave me an appraising look. There was no mistaking the intelligence in his eyes. He then leaned closer and tried to chew one of the buttons on my jacket.

I asked a clerk what kind of parrot I had. "Red belly," was the response.

The price sheet next to the display listed red-bellied parrots for $500. I gently pried the bird from my jacket buttons and put him back on his perch. Scraping up $500 would not be possible any time soon on my salary.

I overheard the clerk telling another clerk that he just loved that "green bird" because she was so sweet. I looked around and finally saw a small green bird sitting on a branch near the back.

"This one," I asked.

The clerk nodded. "Yeah."

She stepped up easily onto my finger. She felt lighter and looked softer than the red belly.

"What kind is this one?"

"She's a brown-head."

I peered at her head; it looked more gray than brown. She made no attempt to climb up my arm or chew on my buttons. Perhaps I had interrupted her nap. I sensed that she was not at all interested in me, and was probably just sitting on my finger to be polite. I gently scritched her head feathers, which she also accepted without much of a response.

The sheet beside the cages listed her as also costing $500.00. I'd have to do more homework, I decided. Then maybe find a breeder who would sell for less.

I gently put her back on the limb. She immediately began preening, indifferent to my presence.

There was very little information on the Internet or in books about the African brown-headed parrot. A subspecies of the poicephalus, the brown-headed parrot was generally considered to be quiet and sweet, but not popular as a pet because they weren't colorful. They were known to talk, too. I joined a Yahoo group dedicated to brown-headed parrots, and the members were patient with my endless questions.

There were three things that convinced me a brown-head would be perfect for me: repeated reports that they were quiet parrots (as far as any parrot is quiet), a picture of a baby brown-head bathing in a bowl of shallow water, and that their eyes would develop rings around their iris as they matured, which gave them a wild appearance. That brown-heads were not run-of-the-mill pet parrots just sealed the deal for me.

Of course, I shared my newfound knowledge with all my friends and with Sugar Franklin, but she did not offer an opinion.

I found a breeder in Louisville who answered all my questions and just happened to have two babies left. I immediately sent the breeder a deposit on the $300 price, and arranged to pick up one of them.

The breeder, David Stearman, put the baby on his kitchen table. The round shape was made of various shades of green feathers with huge black eyes and a long hooked beak. David said the bird was a male and was eating on his own but still enjoyed an occasional syringe feeding.

"Oh, he likes you," David said. David probably said that to all his customers, but I didn't care. I was already in love with the little bundle of soft feathers with those big dark eyes. Who knew that parrots were so endlessly and astonishingly beautiful?

I kept the radio on low during the 90-minute drive home from Louisville. I had already decided to name the brown-head Charlie; it seemed like a friendly name I could see myself calling him. Charlie spent most of the time hanging upside down, staring at me through the bars of the new cage I'd bought for him. Once in a while he would chirp, but his attitude overall was that we were on an adventure and that he was pleased at how things were going. He never gave any indication that I was a stranger or that he had left the only home he'd known.

I stopped at a drive-through restaurant midway for a soft drink and played "Blink" with him. I would blink slowly and Charlie would blink back at me. If I blinked quickly two times, he would blink twice. I hoped no one could see me because it was so absurd, but I was thrilled. It was fun.

He opened and closed his beak at me, rapidly, over and over, as if he were talking with no sound. I didn't know what that meant but assumed the best. When we got home and I put him in his new cage he growled at me. I stepped back. He growled again; no mistaking that for something else.

I let him alone to settle in. I wrote to the Yahoo Brown-Head Parrot list to announce his arrival. One of the women wrote back that the rapidly moving beak meant Charlie was being friendly; the growl meant Charlie was afraid.

I had a few days off so I could keep an eye on him. I called Pennyroyal to have Charlie checked out the next morning.

Dr. Z was not as thrilled as I was. "Where did you get this bird?" she demanded. "Do you know anything about this breeder?" I told her that I felt good about David, had checked him out, and that David had said he was a client of Sam Vaughn, a well-known avian veterinarian in Louisville. Dr. Z immediately called Dr. Vaughn, chatted for a moment, then came back to me.

"Dr. Vaughn said that he runs a clean house," Dr. Z told me. She was more relaxed after the call, so I assumed the best. She listened to Charlie's heart and lungs, examined his throat and ears, examined his feet and beak and wings and feather condition. She didn't think blood work was necessary, and by the end of the exam she seemed pleased.

"Enjoy your new baby," she said. "Don't forget to keep him in quarantine for at least a month," she added.

I had already read and understood that whenever a new bird is introduced to other birds it should be placed away from the other birds in case it is carrying a contagious disease. Often a disease isn't evident in the first week or two, so quarantine is a good way to protect all the birds in the house. I was keeping Charlie in the study, out of sight and reach of Sugar Franklin.

I called David to tell him that Charlie had passed Dr. Z's exam.

David thanked me for letting him know. Almost as an afterthought, he mentioned that Charlie's sister, left alone now, had cried and cried after I'd taken Charlie away.

I felt bad about that and offered to drive back so the two birds could say good-bye properly, but David assured me that wasn't necessary.

Charlie also cried the next few mornings. David had warned me he might regress from the stress of being in a new place. I mixed up the formula David had given me and drew a syringe full. Charlie took it greedily, his enormous eyes on mine as he fed. He refused the syringe during the day and evening, preferring his pellets and vegetables, so I assumed the syringe feeding was more of a comfort measure.

I had read not to give a baby parrot more attention in the beginning than you would have to give normally, so I tried to encourage him to play with toys on a bird stand. Charlie, though, had other ideas, and it soon became impossible for me to ignore his big eyes and his little awkward baby steps climbing down the play stand and trotting across the carpet to get to me. When he was in his cage, he would stand in the corner and flip himself upside down and then chirp at me. Sometimes he got himself tangled up and it would take a few minutes until he figured out how to get his legs and body going in the same direction.

Brown-heads tend to be shy, and most parrots enjoy having a place to hide so I bought a Hide 'n Sleep for his cage. It was a sturdy platform with a support that screwed to the top of the cage and was covered in colorful fabric with just a small opening, like a tent. Charlie immediately began chewing the fabric until it was just so. He didn't like me to touch it after that, and he slept in it every night. I also bought one for Sugar Franklin, but she hissed and fussed so much I finally took it out of her cage. She was happy sleeping high on her cloth perch.

While he was still in quarantine I began training him to step up on command. He did it so naturally and easily that I wondered if I was doing something wrong, but no, Charlie was very smart and immediately understood that hearing "Step up!" meant he was to climb onto my finger and get his little head scritched.

I kept Charlie in the study in quarantine for almost a month. When he would chirp, Sugar Franklin would go into her alert mode. Her crest would stick straight up and she would tighten her feathers around her so she looked skinny. Then she would look at me to check my reaction. After a few days of this she finally relaxed and only turned her head briefly in the direction of the sound. I told her how much she'd like Charlie and that as soon as the 30-day quarantine period was over she could meet him.

The breeder had said brown-heads got along with cockatiels, so I was anxious to introduce Charlie to Sugar Franklin after quarantine. I moved Charlie's cage into the living room, near Sugar's cage. Sugar Franklin was mildly curious, and Charlie just studied her. I knew it would be so much fun to watch them play together.

Even though Dr. Z had told me that, for parrots, a grape was just a bag of sugar water I still offered them to both birds as occasional treats. One evening I had both birds on the couch and placed a peeled grape between them.

They both took tentative nibbles at the grape at the same time, but there was a look in Charlie's eyes I didn't like. He became aggressive about the grape, and his body language told me he didn't like Sugar. I picked him up and let Sugar Franklin finish the grape.

As Charlie grew it became more obvious that he considered Sugar Franklin an enemy. More than once he would start to lunge toward Sugar and I would have to pick him up and move him.

OK, so maybe they weren't going to be best friends.

There were several times I watched Charlie play on the coffee table or floor while Sugar preened on my shoulder. Had I made a mistake in getting Charlie? I pretended to myself that I loved them both equally, but I knew if I had to choose Sugar Franklin would win every time. I tried to give them equal amounts of attention, but Charlie demanded more one-on-one attention than Sugar did. Sugar didn't seem to be jealous of Charlie; he was just an annoyance that got in the way of her getting her own demands met.

He chirped loudly in the mornings and evenings, which was normal for a parrot. There were occasional chirps for attention; otherwise, he was as quiet as I had hoped he would be. He soon taught me that his favorite reward was being petted, not treats.

The breeder told me that Charlie's parents were wild-caught from Tanzania, and I liked to imagine what his life would be like if he had been born there. I pictured him sitting on a tree limb, perhaps preening with a mate or foraging for nuts or seeds, or dipping his beak into a small lake. I wondered what life was like now for his parents, so far from their native land. I felt sure David took good care of them, but I wondered what they thought of their life in captivity. Were they happy to find themselves in such good circumstances where food and water were plentiful and there were no predators to bother them? Or did they sometimes look to the sky and wonder why the sunlight no longer slanted in the same way it did when they were fledglings?

Sugar Franklin, I suspected, had been bred somewhere in town, probably by some woman or man who raised and bred cockatiels as a hobby (I couldn't imagine anyone trying to make a living by breeding cockatiels). She had been under the control of humans all her life and knew nothing about living outside. Once in a while I thought I saw a hint in her eyes of her ancient dinosaur ancestors, or maybe I only imagined that's what I saw.

By the time of Charlie's first annual well-bird exam I thought he was looking a little ragged. The feathers on his chest seemed to be more down feathers than green ones, but I assumed it was just the brown-head version of a normal molt. Brown-heads have brilliant yellow feathers under their wings that you never see unless the bird is in flight. I checked Charlie's yellow feathers and saw that they seemed intact. He absolutely did not like anyone touching his wings, much less lifting them. The chest feathers would improve, I told myself.

Dr. Z quickly corrected me on that. Charlie was plucking out his own feathers. I was shocked. I had heard of parrots plucking out their feathers, but I had assumed they only did this if they weren't receiving good care. I thought I was taking excellent care of my birds.

I explained to Dr. Z where Charlie's cage was placed, we went over his diet of Harrison's adult pellets plus various vegetables and fruits and human foods, how much time he spent out of the cage, and so on. Feather plucking was a mystery to avian vets and parrot owners, Dr. Z told me; no one knew for sure what caused it. She reassured me that I wasn't a "bad" owner because Charlie plucked his feathers. Everything else in the exam and blood work was perfect.

While I was at the clinic, I picked up another bag of Harrison's pellets. When I got home I discovered I had bought the high-potency pellets rather than the regular ones. I had already opened the package, so I couldn't take them back. Charlie ate them without complaint.

I began more research and found that, as usual, Dr. Z had told me the truth. It seemed every other parrot out in the world plucked their feathers. I moved Charlie's cage away from the entry hall in case that was upsetting him. I gave him more baths, which he didn't appreciate. I bought more toys and changed them more frequently.

Slowly his feathers began to grow out. I hoped it had not turned into a habit and that he was finally cured.

The next time I bought pellets I made sure to get the regular ones, which Charlie ate just as readily. To my dismay he began plucking again within a week.

I took Charlie to Dr. Virginia Garrison, the other avian vet in the area. She was known to try homeopathic remedies, and I asked Dr. Z if that would be a good option. Dr. Z approved and didn't seem threatened or concerned about Charlie seeing another veterinarian.

Dr. Garrison's office was closer to my house. I couldn't guess her age, but despite the rumors she had retired, she didn't seem old enough. For several months, Dr. Garrison gave me various compounds that I administered to Charlie. None of them worked.

I had seen advertisements for DNA testing that could determine the gender of parrots. I sent off a tiny bit of Charlie's blood to be tested and was shocked when the results came back that he was really a she. The breeder had been so sure Charlie was a male. I didn't know if that had anything to do with plucking, but I figured any and all information was useful. I immediately changed her name to Charli. My friends were incredulous that such things as DNA tests for parrots not only existed but that just anybody could order one.

One of my favorite writers about parrot behavior was Liz Wilson. Dr. Z also liked what Liz had to say about parrots, and she agreed it would be a good thing to hire Liz to do a phone consultation. I had written to Liz earlier and asked how a person became a parrot behavior consultant. She responded that there were no formal programs, there was no money to be made in the field, and that basically it was a matter of educating myself, going to conferences, and doing hands-on work with parrots.

I also liked that Liz charged a flat fee that included follow-up e-mails for a certain amount of time. Other behaviorists charged hourly fees, and I didn't want to end up spending what might be hundreds or thousands on a problem that might not ever get solved.

Liz e-mailed me a questionnaire that was six pages long. I returned it, along with a video of Charli in her cage, a view of the entire living room from various angles including Sugar Franklin's cage, and of Charli sitting in her cage while I left the house for about 20 minutes. I was curious about what my birds did when I was out of the house, but all Charli did was nap.

Liz's web site information about telephone consultations warned that the initial phone call could last for hours, so I settled in for a nice long chat when it was time for our appointment.

When the time came we talked for less than an hour. She asked me some pointed questions and gave me a few minor suggestions such as getting Charli a larger cage when I could afford it. It turned out, according to Liz, that I seemed to be doing everything right. She reminded me, as had Dr. Z, that we just don't know for certain why birds do this to themselves. She said she would give my situation some more thought and get back with me. I enjoyed talking with Liz and appreciated her candor, but I still had no solutions.

When it was time to buy more Harrison's pellets, the clinic was out of the regular blend so I bought the high-potency again. Within a week or so I could see that Charli was no longer plucking her feathers. It finally dawned on me that there was something in the high-potency blend she needed and wasn't getting in the regular blend.

Liz agreed with me that it was possible the plucking was caused by what she was eating or not eating. Again she reminded me that the causes of plucking are often as varied as the parrots themselves. She suggested I call Harrison's, which I did.

The Harrison's technician I talked with said that the high-potency was recommended for the African species and that African species also often responded well to a bit of red palm oil added to the diet. I didn't want to imagine what would have happened to Charli if I hadn't discovered this. From then on I was careful to only feed her the high-potency Harrison's, along with more fruits and vegetables (most of which she ignored, of course).

Charli liked to ride in the car as much as Sugar Franklin. I now had two small travel cages with extra perches and toys. Any time I was going to be out for most of the day or go out of town I immediately tried to figure out if I could take the birds with me. If travel involved motel rooms, I always checked first if the establishments were pet-friendly and would waive cleaning with chemicals. It did not occur to me that this behavior was unusual; after all, I knew dozens of people over the Internet who were even more crazy than me about their birds. Compared to some of them I was an oasis of sanity.

One afternoon I put both birds in separate small travel cages and drove to my mother's, 70 miles away. I put the birds' cages in the living room so they could watch my mother and me have dinner. I prepared two tiny saucers of our vegetables for the birds, which I put in their cages. They chirped and ignored what I had given them because they wanted what I was eating, which was the exact same thing.

Sugar Franklin chirped her protests so loudly I left the table and opened her cage. She stepped onto my finger and then flew across the room to the table in the dining room. She came to a stop right in the bowl of mashed potatoes. My mother jumped up from her chair. I grabbed the bird and gently wiped her little feet. Then, smiling to myself, I put her back in her cage. Charlie watched all this in silence, but I suspected she was giving Sugar Franklin a parrot smirk.

My mother grabbed the bowl of potatoes and quickly scraped them into the garbage. She put the bowl in the dishwasher, took out a fresh bowl and filled it with the remaining potatoes in the pan.

"Sorry," I said. But I really wasn't.

There were two or three magazines devoted to parrots at that time, and I subscribed to all of them. When one of them invited articles about the poicephalus species, I wrote a short piece about the African brown-headed parrot for the poicephalus species issue, which was published. It was the first non-work-related thing I had written since I began working at the hospital.

I had a poetry manuscript from graduate school no one seemed interested in publishing, and my work environment drained me so much I had given up on writing anything creative again. The simple act of writing the article about the African brown-headed parrot gave me hope again.

Chapter Six

I was sound asleep when I heard a rustle from Sugar Franklin's cage. I woke up immediately and jumped out of bed. There was a louder sound of wings and crush of paper. I flipped up the towel covering her cage.

"What's the matter, sweetie," I whispered.

She was bent low on her perch, hissing, her crest high and tight. She lifted her wings from her body, making herself huge. She was focused on something in the cage.

There was very little light in the living room so it took me a few moments before I saw what the commotion was about. A tiny mouse was in the cage, terrified into motionlessness as Sugar began to sway a little, back and forth.

A mouse? In my house? I tried to think what to do. The mouse ran to the side of the cage; Sugar swayed more and hissed again.

I got a paper bag, opened the cage door, and tried to angle the opening of the bag inside the cage. The mouse, which I thought would eagerly run right into the bag, sped to the other side of the cage.

I was terrified of touching the mouse but more terrified that the mouse might hurt Sugar Franklin. She was certainly intimidating but I didn't know what the mouse might be capable of. What if it were carrying some awful disease?

After several more tries I captured the mouse in the bag. Holding the bag as far away from me as possible, I ventured outside in my nightgown. I walked down the block to the nearest intersection, bent down and opened the bag, and watched the mouse scamper away. Please don't come back, I told it in my mind.

When I returned Sugar Franklin had settled back on her perch and was asleep, as if nothing had happened. I uncovered Charli's cage to be sure it was mouse-free. Charli poked her head out of her Hide n' Sleep. I threw away the paper bag and went back to bed to lie awake imagining I heard mice in the walls, on the floors, in the ceiling. It was three in the morning.

I never left food out overnight, so the mouse must have been attracted by the pellets in Sugar Franklin's and Charli's cages. I checked with my Internet parrot friends, who all seemed to have had similar experiences with mice. Over the next several weeks I set out humane mice traps, but they never caught any mice. I knew they were there because I could see an occasional dropping. Finally I called the local "green" pest control company.

He examined my house, inside and out, then finally gave me the verdict. "Your house is wide open," he said. "There are openings under the siding where they're coming in. There's no point in me doing anything until you get those fixed."

We discussed traps; he said he was all in favor of the humane traps except that they didn't work. What I needed were the old-fashioned Victor spring traps, baited with peanut butter. "Mice just can't resist peanut butter," he told me.

The weather was getting cold, but I made several inspections of the siding and foundation. I couldn't see any cracks, and my fingers were too cold to feel anything out of the ordinary, if I had even known what was ordinary to begin with. I had no idea who to call or trust to check the situation for me and do what was needed. It would, I already knew, cost far more than I was willing to pay. Maybe once I got my credit cards paid off, I told myself.

I set traps in every room of the house. The snap of the spring slipping from the catch would wake me up, and in the mornings I would pick up the trap and dead mouse with a paper towel, put them in a paper bag, and throw out the paper bag. I killed about four mice over a period of a few months, and I hated it more each time.

Chapter Seven

Late one Friday afternoon I was trying to get the laundry caught up when I heard a yelp of pain from Sugar Franklin.

I rushed to her cage and was horrified to see blood on her wing. I scooped her up. One of her feathers had broken and blood was dripping down her feathers. She bent to touch the feather with her beak and squawked with pain.

The books and the Internet postings of friends I'd read made it clear that Sugar Franklin could die if the bleeding didn't stop. Cockatiels didn't have that much blood to being with. I called Pennyroyal and told one of the techs what had happened.

"It's probably okay," she said calmly. "Just watch her. If it gets worse, call us back, but I imagine it's okay."

"Should I try to pull it?"

"No, just leave her alone and see what happens."

I put down the phone. I couldn't be sure but the area of blood didn't seem to be growing. I took Sugar into the bathroom and tried to clean off the blood with some water and a washcloth, but she bit me if I tried to get near the broken feather.

I put her back in her cage. She calmly went to her food dish and examined it carefully in case some treats had magically appeared. I found a bag of Nutriberries and put three in her food dish, which she ate calmly as if she'd just ordered them in a restaurant. The bleeding seemed to have stopped. Or maybe it was just my imagination.

On Friday nights, I usually had dinner with a couple of friends from work, but there was no way I was going to leave Sugar Franklin alone. I was not going to risk coming home to a dead bird. My friends laughed when I called to cancel our plans but said they understood.

While I watched television that night Sugar Franklin preened herself, took a drink of water, and ate more Nutriberries and pellets as if nothing had happened. After an hour or so, she reached behind her and began working at the broken blood feather. Within a few minutes, without any fuss, she had managed to work the broken feather loose and yank it out. She dropped it out of her mouth and walked away from it, as if it were so much trash.

She ignored me when I opened her cage and removed the broken feather. The blood had clotted at the broken place and the end of the shaft had been pulled out neatly and cleanly.

When no more blood appeared and she continued to behave normally, I finally relaxed.

Dr. Z later told me horror stories of well-meaning owners using pliers to pull broken blood feathers only to rip out flesh along with the feather. Sugar Franklin had taken care of things herself so I wouldn't have to. I couldn't think of a human being I admired more than I admired Sugar Franklin at that moment for her courage and calm in doing what needed to be done.

I put some more Nutriberries in her food dish.

I was becoming aware of all the terrible things that could happen to a parrot. What if Sugar Franklin somehow flew out the door or window? I had read that often a parrot can fly miles in that first flush of fear and adrenaline, and then not recognize where they are, much less be able to find their way home. What if she were attacked by a cat or a dog or a hawk, left injured to bleed to death? Or starve because she couldn't recognize what was safe to eat outside? What if some stranger found her and put her in a tiny cage and ignored her or had mean children who would poke her with sticks? Or wouldn't give her vet care if she were ill or give her any attention or yell at her for screaming or lock her in a cold dark basement?

During these times I would pick her up and scritch her head and talk softly to her about how much I loved her and that I would never let anything awful happen to her. Was it possible, I wondered, to live an entire life free of fear and any pain worse than a broken blood feather? I doubted it was possible for humans, but perhaps it was possible for parrots. Sugar Franklin deserved no less.

About this time I noticed Sugar Franklin doing what many parrot owners call the "skirt dance." She would puff out her feathers and slowly walk in a circle, giving out soft chirps. She would then back up to the rim of one of her food dishes and rub her vent against it for several minutes, then stop and go on about her business as if nothing interesting was going on. I ignored the behavior, only telling her once to be sure not to do it in front of my mother or friends.

A few months later I was working in the study with Sugar in her usual place on my left shoulder. She had been unusually quiet that morning, and I was grateful she wasn't driving me crazy running all over the desk. In fact, I had forgotten she was on my shoulder when I felt something hot on my arm. I looked over just in time to see a small, perfectly formed egg sliding down my skin. I grabbed it before it fell to the desk. It was hot and wet.

"Sugar!" I said. "Look what you did!"

Sugar Franklin glanced at the egg then began preening her wing. I held up the egg to her, but she was not the least bit interested.

"You laid an egg!" I couldn't contain my astonishment.

Nothing I said or did with the egg interested her. I could almost hear her thinking that it certainly had nothing whatsoever to do with her. She glanced at it, then went back to her feathers.

I called my mother with the news.

My mother asked, "I thought there had to be a male around."

"No," I explained. "It just won't hatch because there's no male around."

"Ah," my mother said, as if she understood perfectly.

I wrote to Tiel Talk. Everyone had advice for me: I should limit the amount of daylight she received. Or increase the amount. I should not feed her soft warm foods, but I should feed her foods with extra calcium. I was warned repeatedly to watch out for excessive egg laying, but Sugar didn't lay another egg for a couple of weeks.

I became paranoid about her laying eggs at all. I called Pennyroyal for advice and was told Sugar Franklin could be given a series of some sort of hormone injections that would most likely stop her from laying eggs at all. Dr. Z agreed the injections would be prudent, but she also reminded me that Sugar Franklin was healthy and I didn't need to worry too much about excessive egg laying unless she began laying eggs non-stop.

Sugar laid a few more eggs that season and showed no interest in them. The following year she began laying more eggs and, I decided to have Sugar Franklin take the series of injections. There was no point in risking her laying too many eggs.

Sugar Franklin stopped laying eggs for over two years with no ill effects, but she continued to masturbate regularly on her food dishes. During these times she would begin investigating any dark places she could find -- under a sheet of paper, small spaces between two items on the coffee table, a corner of the sofa. I would drag her away from her explorations, getting bitten for my trouble. I didn't want to do anything that would encourage her to make a nest and lay eggs.

Chapter Eight

According to Pennyroyal there was a bird club in
town that met once a month in a building on the
university campus. I attended a few meetings, but
there were never more than five people at a time at
any meeting. They did, however, hold a big bird fair
every autumn in the National Guard Armory.

I was late getting to the bird show and was
glad to see that the armory was crowded with
people and vendors. I scribbled my name on the list
and introduced myself to the woman in charge of the
table.

"Are you a club member?" she asked.

"Absolutely!" I said.

"Oh good. Do you have birds?"

"I've got a cockatiel and a brown-head," I
said. We easily fell into the usual chitchat about
parrots that parrot owners repeat all over the world.
Species and numbers of parrots being more
important than human information.

"Now don't let me buy a bird," I said, and we
both laughed. I looked around at all the cages of
parrots, some of them hanging out on top of their
cages. I was prepared to buy lots of toys and treats,
but I knew I had to be strong when it came to
another bird. "I've barely got room for the ones I've
got now." Between the human conversations and
squawks of parrots I doubted she heard me.

I went off to investigate new toys and treats.
Sugar Franklin never seemed interested in toys, so I
was always searching for something bright and
colorful she couldn't resist but not so big as to

overpower her. I found several small safe chewable toys for her and several larger toys for Charli. I imagined the birds being so excited at the new toys and eager to play with them -- it was a fantasy I had many times.

Some vendors offered seed, pellets, nuts, treats. Other vendors displayed handmade toys of leather and rope, toy-making supplies, and all kinds of supplies. Water bottles; food dishes; talking mirrors; toys that would play songs if the bird pushed a certain button; perches of cloth, wood, and sand-covered. There was a huge assortment of cages in every size, as well as play stands, cage cleaners, special cage liner papers, and even necklaces for humans to wear that the parrot could then chew to bits.

There were several drawings for many of the items, and I bought a lot of tickets to stuff into the drawing boxes.

Anyone wanting a bird could find one that day. Green amazons, huge blue & gold macaws flapping their wings and screaming, white cockatoos bowing their heads for scritches, blue and green parrotlets ready to bite any finger foolish enough to approach, brilliant conures screeching.

Near the exit were several small bird breeders; finches, canaries, parakeets, and cockatiels. I stopped to watch two cockatiels in one cage for a bit. The man behind the table began telling me that the cockatiels had been bred by a friend who had since died. He was selling them because he didn't know anything cockatiels; he raised finches.

A small gray cockatiel clung to the front of the cage and watched me. "That's a good one," the man said, nodding at the bird. "A bargain at $75. The other one's already been sold."

"Thanks, but no," I said. "No more birds for me!"

"I've got to sell him," the man went on as if I hadn't said a word. "How about $50?"

I shook my head. "I've only got five bucks on me." After buying toys and treats I felt lucky to have that much money left. I was also pleased with myself that there was no possibility of me buying a bird.

I moved back to the sign-in table for a while to watch people come and go.

"There's the cutest little cockatiel over there," I told the woman at the table.

"You're not supposed to buy a bird," she laughed.

"Oh no," I said. "I was just looking. Besides, I don't have a cage or anything to put a bird in."

More visitors came in. I went back to look at the two cockatiels again. The same gray cockatiel was now alone in the cage; he climbed to the front of the cage and clung to the bars.

"That's a good bird," the man said. "He's about 6 months old."

The cockatiel was watching me with those big dark baby eyes.

"He plays with his toys," the man went on. "My granddaughter feeds him Cheerios every night."

I could picture feeding this bird Cheerios, one at time. If he played with toys maybe he could convince Sugar to play with toys. Would he and

Sugar Franklin get along? What if he turned out to be a male and they had babies? What if they hated one another? Was the extra cage clean?

"No," I said. "No money. Sorry."

"I tell you what, I'll take a check."

"I didn't bring my checkbook, and I've only got five bucks on me."

"You can just mail me a check. I'm not taking him home," he added.

What was wrong with this man, to not take this bird home? What was he going to do, set it free to starve or get eaten by a hawk? Leave it at the armory?

The cockatiel clung to the front of the cage, watching me. "I don't have anything to take him home in," I said.

"I'll find you a box." The man jumped up and began rummaging under the table. He grabbed the cockatiel and dropped him into the box, which had a torn flap. "You've got a good one," he said again.

He took my five-dollar bill and gave me his business card.

I turned to see the woman at the table staring at me. I shrugged and lifted the box. So much for not buying another bird.

The new bird went into the study for quarantine until I could get him to Pennyroyal to be checked out. I'd read enough horror stories of people bringing home new birds only to lose both old and new birds to contagious diseases.

I decided to wait and allow a suitable name for the new bird to come to me. He quickly learned his step-ups, and I saw for the first time that his beak was crooked. It didn't affect his ability to eat or drink but it did give him a snarling expression. His sweet disposition cancelled out his appearance.

The second day I was with him in my study when something startled him. He instinctively lifted his wings and flew across the room, like a flash of light.

"Flash," I thought. "That's his name. Flash."

Sugar Franklin and Charli were curious about the new bird noises coming from the study, and I explained to them that we had a new friend in the house. They did not seem impressed.

Dr. Z was not overly impressed either when I told her the story of how I came to have a new bird. She checked him over and took blood and a sample of his poop for testing. The next day she called with the news that he tested positive for chlamydia. Chlamydia is also known as psittacosis or parrot fever; it is very common and one of the few diseases that can be transmitted from parrot to human. To protect Sugar Franklin and Charli I would have to have all three of them treated with several rounds of injections. Even though Flash was in quarantine, we all shared the same ventilation system.

Chlamydia is highly contagious, and I thought the man who had sold me Flash would want to know his flock was infected. When I called and told him about Flash, he denied that any of his birds were sick.

"I'd know if they were sick," he said. "I don't have to waste money at the vet's for that."

"But you wouldn't know they were sick until it's too late," I said. "And psittacosis is something humans can get from birds."

"All my birds are healthy." He slammed down the phone. I stood there, feeling like a fool.

I told Dr. Z about my conversation. She was unsurprised. "That's what a lot of breeders think. Until their birds start dying or their grandkids get sick."

Since all three birds were being treated for Flash's psittacosis there wasn't much point in continuing quarantine. I introduced Flash to Sugar Franklin first.

"See," I told her, holding Flash up for her inspection. "This is Flash. He's a little younger than you, but that's a good thing."

Sugar Franklin was standing on top of her cage and eyed him carefully. Flash tried to climb down my hand toward her, so I let him hop onto the cage top. Sugar lowered her crest and hissed at him.

He walked toward her but stopped a respectable distance away. Sugar lowered her head and hissed again. Flash cocked his head to the side but didn't move.

Sugar Franklin's expression was unmistakable.

"Come on," I said to her. "You two could be great friends. Why, you might even like having sex with him. Wouldn't you like to have some baby cockatiels?"

Sugar hissed again at him, then turned back to me.

"All right," I sighed. I picked up Flash and sat on the couch with him for a little while. We practiced step-ups, and he reluctantly accepted scritches.

"You're so cute," I told him. "Sugar Franklin is just being difficult. Let's just give her some time, okay?"

Chapter Nine

My first parrot conference. I normally didn't like going to conferences because all the work-related ones I'd attended were boring beyond belief. But this was different. This would be full of parrot lovers like me. I didn't even mind that it was in Minnesota.

Of course I had to find someone to bird sit while I was gone. Normally I would ask one of the techs at Pennyroyal to bird sit for me; they were familiar with my birds, knew what an avian emergency was, and were willing to bird sit for the small amount I could afford to pay. However, that spring none of the techs were available so I had to find someone new. It would have to be someone who was responsible and had experience with birds and knew how to play with parrots and be trusted not to give the birds the wrong foods.

One of the Pennyroyal techs told me about a wild life rehabilitator who lived nearby, so I contacted her. We found we had friends in common, so I began to feel hopeful. She warned me she didn't have time to wash cages or do any cooking for the birds, which I hadn't even considered. Otherwise, she agreed to come to my house twice a day to be sure they had ample food and water, give them attention, and generally make sure everything was as it should be.

I arrived in Minnesota a day early so I could spend an entire day at the Mall of America. That night, before the welcoming cocktail party, I called the bird sitter to be sure she'd gotten into my house all right and that everything was fine. She reassured me everyone had been fed and played with and that I didn't need to worry.

There were several seminars I wanted to attend, such as the importance of toys for parrots, signs of illness in parrots, a video of a parrot pair caring for their young in the nest, and so on. There were too many to attend them all.

I found Liz Wilson and introduced myself to her, after reminding her of our phone consultation about Charli. She asked after Charli and Dr. Z and then introduced me to some people who I promptly forgot.

The second morning I was having breakfast in the hotel when Liz and Phoebe Linden and a couple of other women walked by. We all smiled at one another, then Liz waved me over to join them.

I couldn't believe my luck -- Liz Wilson and Phoebe Linden! Phoebe was famous for her theory of abundance weaning; basically, allowing chicks to wean on their own individual schedules rather than forcing them onto adult foods at set times. She was also a highly respected parrot breeder in Santa Barbara, California, and well-known author.

They were friendly and interested in anything I had to say. I had never dreamed I would be so close to such celebrities who would actually care to listen to anything I had to say.

A roundtable discussion that afternoon featuring both Liz and Phoebe included a question and answer section. Somehow Phoebe got on the subject of providing foraging toys and plants for parrots.

"Get a fichus tree," she told us. "They're not that expensive and you can keep them indoors. Go to Home Depot or Lowe's. Parrots love playing on trees."

A fichus tree? What a wonderful idea! I could just imagine Sugar Franklin and Charli and Flash cavorting in the leaves in the living room and all the wonderful pictures I could take of them. I immediately resolved to check out the fichus tree situation when I got home.

I bought tee shirts from the World Parrot Trust and Gabriel Foundation. I entered all the raffles and I bought lots of toys and books and treats for the birds. I went back to the Mall of America for one last go-around.

When I got home the birds seemed glad to see me but, as usual, were not interested in any of the toys or treats I'd bought for them. Remembering Phoebe's talk, I made trips to Home Depot and Lowe's, searching for just the right size fichus tree that would fit in my living room. All I could find were insubstantial plants or trees too big for indoors. Finally I came across a crooked fichus tree small enough for my house and took it home.

The birds were terrified of it. I gently placed Sugar Franklin on one of the branches and praised her for trying it out. She was not fooled and insisted on jumping back to my shoulder. Flash responded the same way, only he hissed mightily at the sight of it.

Charli leaned so far away from the tree that she nearly fell off my hand. When I tried to have her step onto a branch, she refused to leave my finger. Nothing would induce her to go near it.

They just needed time, I told myself. I would point out the tree to them several times a day, pet the leaves, and talk about how much fun it would be to perch on the branches. The only creature I impressed was myself.

After a week or two, the fichus tree had lost most of its leaves. The birds continued to view it as some sort of sleeping monster that might awaken at any time.

I wrote a long e-mail to Liz and Phoebe about the "adventure" I'd been having with the fichus tree and how I had finally given up and put it on the back deck to finish dying.

"You should publish this," Phoebe wrote me. I laughed and wrote back, "Who on earth would publish it?"

"Talk to Carla Thornton at parrotchronicles.com. You could even start writing a column or something," came the immediate answer.

Carla was polite but not overly enthusiastic. Did I have anything else to show her? I sent her a couple of ideas and she finally agreed to give me a chance. It wouldn't pay much, she warned. Pay? It had not occurred to me I would get paid.

She suggested the title of the column be "A Bird in Hand." Would that be all right?

That was fine with me. I just hoped I could live up to the rigors of being a columnist plus being funny at the same time. Writers like Dave Barry made it look so easy, but I knew better.

My second column was about the experience of finding a bird sitter who warned me she didn't have time to clean the cages or cook for my birds.

The third column was about Paris Hilton and Nicole Richie having a "real life" episode with parrots. I thought the idea was hilarious, but I couldn't make it funny on paper. Carla made some changes that made it very funny indeed.

I began to get comments from readers about my columns. I loved reading and answering their questions and comments. Perhaps I had found a new career as a humor writer. I immediately began fantasizing of being able to leave my job and embark on a lifetime of spreading joy to the world of parrot owners.

Carla and I soon found a nice rhythm; I would send her my column and she would either suggest very minor changes or just make the changes and send them back for approval. She never made any suggestions or changes that didn't greatly improve the column. I slowly gave up the dream of becoming America's great parrot humorist because I knew I lacked Carla's gift of adding the bon mot that always made the column sparkle.

I wrote a few non-humor articles for parrotchronicles.com as well, but I loved the challenge of coming up with new ideas for "A Bird in the Hand."

Chapter Ten

I took a deep breath and pressed the Enter key to send the e-mail to Liz. Would she, I asked, consider being my mentor? Since there were no programs to teach me what I needed to know it seemed a mentor/protégé approach was my only option. I had had Sugar Franklin for about five years and was confronted more every day with just how little I knew.

Liz and I had been writing each other regularly since the conference, and I liked what she had to say about parrots and parrot owners and the importance of plain common sense. I could certainly choose worse.

While I had broad streaks of knowledge about parrots, I needed to learn more. Liz could help me piece together what I knew with what I still needed to learn.

She responded almost immediately that she would be pleased to teach me. She sent me a list of books to read as a beginning. I felt proud of myself for having already read most of them. In the months that followed Liz and I kept up a steady stream of e-mails, and she included me in numerous discussions with other parrot behavior consultants.

I also needed hands-on experience. I told Dr. Z that I was learning to become a parrot behavior consultant, and she sent me my first client, a woman with a pair of cockatiels who were sitting on a bumper crop of eggs.

She lived in a small apartment, and about a third of her living room was devoted to the two gray cockatiels. Two cages were set up with a walkway between them. The owner was concerned about all the eggs the hen was laying and then, later, what to do with all the babies. The hen, she said, would only come out once a day and was very aggressive about the nest. I explained that the behaviors sounded normal and made some suggestions to enhance the birds' diet, especially to increase calcium for the hen.

If the eggs hatched the chicks could probably be sold to a pet store or given to friends. Or, if she fell in love with them, she could keep them, I told her.

I also explained that the male banging his beak on the cages was not a sign of aggression but a normal male behavior; he was simply demonstrating his ownership of the space.

Because I was still a novice I didn't charge for consultations for over a year. I wasn't sure I knew enough to be worth paying, and I knew I still needed a lot more experience with a variety of birds before I would feel confident about charging.

There were times clients had questions I couldn't answer or when I forgot to mention something important. I would have to research and call them back with the information.

I sent a report to Dr. Z or whichever other veterinarian had sent me a client. I also wrote Liz about each consultation. She would point out what I had done well, what I needed to improve, with suggestions of how to correct problems.

I learned that most people I met had problems with their parrot because they simply didn't know how much time and attention a parrot needs. Those were the people too busy to be bothered to learn about their bird or who wanted me to give them a quick fix.

Most unfortunate for the birds were owners who weren't actually interested in solving problems. They could then say they had tried everything, including consultations with a "parrot expert." In one case, a man wanted his macaw devoiced because he didn't like how loud the bird was; his vet had suggested he meet with me to find other solutions. There were several things I suggested that would have helped the situation, but the owner didn't want to do any of them. In another case, a client tried to give me the bird he had had for eleven years so he and his family could travel across the country in their RV with their new dog.

Fortunately, most of my clients loved their parrots and considered them a permanent part of the family. My favorite consultations were with owners of new parrots; they were excited and determined to learn all they could and to start out on the right foot. They paid attention to what I had to say and followed my suggestions.

I met Christine when she called me about her umbrella cockatoo, named George. She worked in a vet clinic and someone had dropped off the bird and asked them to find George a new home. Christine was a friendly woman with an easy laugh; she had never had a bird before. She just knew that George belonged with her. She'd never felt this way about an animal, she told me, but she was now afraid she was in over her head.

When I arrived at her house I went over some basics about cockatoos and parrots in general, recommended she have Dr. Z check out George, and encouraged her to call me if she had questions. "Working with a parrot is a process," I always told my clients. "There are no quick fixes, and problems are not going to be solved overnight."

Christine called me two days later, in tears. What if she'd made a horrible mistake? What if she couldn't make George happy? What if she couldn't control him?

I told her that we don't really know what makes a parrot "happy," so she should mark that one off her worry list. We know how to provide a decent diet and environment, so we work from there. As for controlling him, I asked her to remember what her children had been like when they were toddlers. "That's your bird's emotional level. Think of George as a toddler and you won't have to worry about controlling him." I offered to come over and show her again how to teach George to step up.

"What if he bites me?" she asked.

I considered lying but decided against it. "Oh, he'll probably bite you sooner or later," I told her. "The important thing is how you respond. Gently tell him 'no,' put him on his perch, and ignore him for a few minutes. If you scream or jump up and down or shake your finger in his face, he'll just consider that drama. Parrots love drama, and they don't care if it's negative or positive. If they can get a dramatic response from you they'll repeat the behavior in order to get you to act that way again."

Christine called again in a few weeks. Dr. Z had determined that George was probably wild caught and perhaps over 25 years old. He had blocked arteries and arthritis, "like a little old man," Christine said. He adored Christine above all else, and she reciprocated by lavishing him with attention and toys and special foods. He tolerated Christine's husband and children, but only because Christine thought them valuable.

There was a job opening for a receptionist at Pennyroyal, and Christine applied and was hired. She and I soon became fast friends.

Podcasts were just becoming known in the Internet world. I had a Macintosh computer and GarageBand software, so I rigged up a system to record phone conversations with various people in the parrot world. I figured I could offer the podcasts for free, sell ads on a website, and get rich. Liz agreed to be my first interviewee, followed by such experts as Diane Grindol on cockatiels, Dr. Harrison of Harrison's Bird Foods, Kashmir Csaky on hyacinth macaws, Dr. Jonathan Reyman about his feather donation program, Steve Milpacher of the World Parrot Trust, Laura Moore of the National Center for Animal Law, and so on.

After a couple of years with absolutely no income from the podcast website I finally accepted that I wasn't going to get rich this way and would have to continue working at the university.

Partly because of the podcasts and partly because Liz wrote a monthly column for *Bird Talk*, my name came to the attention of the magazine's editors. They asked if I'd be interested in writing some articles about the latest uses of technology that could benefit birds. They didn't have to ask twice.

I loved writing for *Parrot Chronicles*, but *Bird Talk* was a commercial publication read by millions of bird lovers. As far as I was concerned, writing those articles for them made me, at long last, a legitimate "real" writer. However, they did not have enough assignments to enable me to make a living at it.

A year or so later, Christine came up with the idea of a website where people could post pictures of their parrots with funny captions. This, we decided, would be our ticket to easy, fabulous wealth. We set up a site, and when the pictures came in Christine would add a silly caption and I would post it. This endeavor, while a lot of fun, didn't make any money either, and we closed the site after a year.

Chapter Eleven

Pennyroyal almost always had a small caged songbird in their lobby, usually a canary but occasionally another species. One day, a few months after their canary Puccini had died, a gray cockatiel was in the cage. There was something odd about his feathers; they were curled and ragged. I knew Dr. Z wouldn't put a bird in the lobby that was carrying something contagious, but there was clearly something wrong with the cockatiel.

One of the techs told me the bird was a rescue named Nicholas. The curled feathers, she said, were just one of the signs of neglect the bird had been through.

Except for his feathers he was a handsome cockatiel. When he saw Sugar Franklin arrive for her well-bird exam, he began calling to her, clinging to the front of the cage. Sugar, of course, ignored these declarations of admiration, but I was secretly pleased.

After the exam, I paid the bill and took Sugar Franklin out to the car. Nicholas continued to call and call, his strident voice clear even in the parking lot. Sugar Franklin gave no indication that she had heard him at all.

"I think he likes you," I told her. "You could at least have acknowledged him." Sugar began preening and ignored me.

Stopping by the clinic occasionally to buy more pellets or having bird wings or nails trimmed, I noticed that after several months Nicholas' curly feathers had been replaced with sleek shiny healthy ones. He was always friendly and happy to greet both humans and animals to the clinic. Whenever I brought Sugar in, Nicholas would call and call for her.

It was obvious to me that the poor thing was always devastated to see us leave. Sugar was a heartbreaker, no question about it.

Liz and I had been corresponding for a long time, and I considered her a friend but lately there were times she and I argued. It seemed to me that the arguments were becoming more frequent. The last straw was when I made an off-handed remark about what parrots ate in the rainforest. Liz pointed out that no one really knew what parrots ate in the rainforest because no one had actually recorded and weighed exactly what went into their beaks and what came out their vents, and until that happened I had no business stating that I knew what parrots in the rainforest ate. I found this criticism ridiculous and told her so. I knew I would never know as much about parrots as Liz, but I wasn't going to tolerate such bizarre criticisms. Though after I had thought about it for a while I realized she was right.

About a year after rescuing Flash, Dr. Garrison, who now worked at Pennyroyal a few days a week to help Dr. Z with the avian clients, came out to the lobby and asked if I'd like to have Nicholas. He needed a home, she said, some place more stable and quiet than the clinic. He was, she said, kind of loud.

I didn't really want another bird, but Nicholas was, after all, so obviously in love with Sugar Franklin. Things weren't working out friendship-wise between Sugar and Flash; maybe she'd warm up to Nicholas if they were together more. He wouldn't be so loud if he was in the same room as Sugar Franklin, I reasoned.

Dr. Garrison and the tech explained that he had been rescued from a woman who had used him as a breeder. Before coming to the clinic, his cage hadn't been cleaned in months, everyone in the house smoked, and he'd lived on a seed and potato chip diet. He was so underweight when he was rescued that he wasn't expected to live. That helped explain the curly feathers. He was 16 years old, had been converted to Harrison's pellets, and except for still being underweight he was healthy -- against all the odds.

Sixteen seemed old for a cockatiel, especially one that had been through as much as Nicholas. On the other hand, I had just heard of a cockatiel that lived to be 35, so maybe Nicholas would be one who lived into his 30s, too.

The tech put him in his original, now clean cage, along with a bright pink rubbery hanging toy that had come with him "so he'll have something familiar."

I wasn't worried about quarantine since Dr. Garrison had said Nicholas had a clean bill of health. I would put him into one of my old cages and place that on top of Flash's cage. It wasn't the best arrangement, but it would do until I figured something else out.

As soon as we walked in to my house, Nicholas began calling and shrieking. It was obvious he was thrilled to be with other birds. He frequently sang a broken version of the wolf whistle that always ended with more calling and shrieking. Sometimes he wailed in the evenings, as if keening, and Charli would chirp out a loud rebuke that only silenced him for a few minutes.

Nicholas was a scritch addict. Every time he saw me, he lowered his head and turned his eyes up to see if I would pet him. He was very specific about it, too. I was allowed to scritch his head and around his ears, but he didn't like his crest or neck touched, and he would nip me immediately if I forgot.

Flash seemed to resent Nicholas and began refusing to let me touch him. Nicholas followed him around like a devoted little brother. I hoped it was just a matter of time before they became best buds, and maybe then Flash would let me scritch him again.

On days when I let the cockatiels out of their cages the boys would run over to Sugar Franklin's cage. She automatically came to me, and we would watch the boys rummage through her cage, drinking her water and eating her pellets, which were the same as theirs, as if they were starved. Then they would look around the cage, surprised that Sugar was no longer in it.

Nicholas would stand at the cage door and sing to Sugar Franklin. She would listen then turn her attention back to me. Flash knew from experience Sugar wasn't interested in masculine company so he no longer puffed out his wings or strutted back and forth in front of her.

I felt sorry for the male cockatiels. Sugar Franklin obviously believed herself to be a superior version of a human and that was my fault. I had spoiled her so much she could never think of herself as a mere bird.

Doing parrot consultations and being involved in the parrot world had helped improve my self-confidence as time went on. Despite my unhappiness with my job, parrots had opened up an endlessly intriguing aspect of life I could have never imagined. They made bearable what had been unbearable.

I even found the courage to join a women's community chorus that gave formal performances twice a year. We rehearsed every Sunday evening in a church near my house. Singing with a group was a joy I hadn't indulged in since high school, and I soon made more new friends.

After one of the rehearsals several of us went to a local Mexican restaurant for a late supper. After our table had shared several pitchers of beer, one of the sopranos began singing the slow version of Neil Sedaka's *Breaking Up is Hard to Do*. I and the rest of our table joined in. Then we sang the fast version, and a few people at nearby tables applauded when we had finished. Later, a man walked over, placed a dollar bill in front of the soprano, and said he'd never had such an entertaining meal in a restaurant.

I began to play more music and sing more at home. The birds seemed to like classical music, but they watched me warily whenever I sang to them.

Bev was another friend I made because of parrots. She was a grad student at the university and was considering getting a small parrot. She wrote me one day, asking if I knew about a group of people in Indiana who took in abandoned parrots and made unannounced visits to homes of people who had adopted their birds. I didn't know the group, but I agreed with them in principle.

When I met Bev she was holding an almost life-sized blue and gold robotic macaw. She called him Squawkers, and I soon learned that she took him everywhere with her. He spoke random phrases as well as playing back recorded sentences and sounds. We all behaved as if Squawkers was as real as any live parrot, only without the poop.

Bev decided to adopt two little gray cockatiels she named Dylan and Brubaker. I helped her and her partner Marty get the birds out of the cage and onto the women's fingers. I loved the delight on their faces when the birds first agreed to sit on their outstretched fingers. They were well on their way to becoming what I called "good parrot slaves."

Almost a year after joining the chorus I decided to take piano lessons from our pianist, Oxana. She was a dark beautiful woman from Russia who held several advanced degrees in music from her homeland. We would meet in the same church where the chorus rehearsed, and Oxana would fuss at me when I did not practice well enough or did not learn what I was supposed to learn.

I did not have a piano at home, but I did have an old electronic keyboard I used for practice. I would put Sugar Franklin on my shoulder and begin my keyboard exercises. Sometimes Sugar would chirp in my ear if she liked what I was doing, or bite my ear if she didn't. Most of the time, though, she was content to sit still and listen. She was careful not to climb off my shoulder and stand on the keys because she didn't understand which keys would make noises and which ones wouldn't.

Chapter Twelve

In the spring of 2009 Sugar Franklin began laying a lot of eggs again. After the first egg, each one she laid was smaller than the last. I finally took her to Pennyroyal on Thursday before the Memorial Day holiday for a lupron injection. There were rumors that Dr. Z was planning to sell the clinic and move, but in the meantime she had hired another veterinarian fresh from school. Dr. Sonia Lacki was a young and gentle woman, but she gave Sugar the lepton injection quickly and efficiently.

Sugar Franklin accepted this with her usual indignation and fussing but settled down once she was back home in her cage. She refused to come out for several hours. When she did she immediately began looking for dark places to nest in, and hissed at me when I moved her away back into the light.

She would hold marathon masturbation sessions so I began removing her favorite dishes from her cage. Later in the night, when she was finally asleep, I would put the dishes back.

"You need to see this abused bird on Tiel Talk," AL wrote me one morning. "This woman in South Africa rescued it."

"No," I wrote back immediately. "I don't want to see another abused bird as long as I live." Stories and pictures of abused and neglected parrots were nearly as plentiful on the Internet as dogs or cats; there was no way to avoid them.

There is a standing joke among parrot owners called MBS, which stands for multiple bird syndrome, the inability to resist getting another parrot. Once you have one parrot you naturally want another. Sometimes, though, one more parrot was one too many for someone's home or budget or lifestyle. We all knew stories of hoarding and had heard of suspect "rescues" that were only an excuse for a hoarder to obtain more birds.

By the end of the day my curiosity got the best of me. I scrolled down the Tiel Talk board and there it was -- a picture of a lutino cockatiel just like Sugar Franklin on a perch with its entire belly covered with what looked like blood. Her right foot was swollen to about twice the size of her left. I took a deep breath and began to read the posts.

The bird had been in a pet store, with no food or water. The owner of the pet store just shrugged and said she had been in a fight with her cage mate, another cockatiel. The cage mate was huddled up in the corner with no blood on him, so the rescuer (LC) knew there had been no fight. Then she saw the injured bird's foot; it had been severed nearly through. She grabbed the bird out of the cage and ran to the car with her, leaving her husband to pay. She heard the pet store owner laughing as she fled.

Her regular vet was not available until the next day, so LC took the injured bird home and attempted to disinfect the cut foot and stop the bleeding. She saw that the bird had no feathers on her head or neck. The bird could not eat or drink, so LC tried to force feed her and then just held her against her chest all night to keep her warm.

The next morning the veterinarian found that the little cockatiel was not only completely dehydrated but also had diarrhea and pneumonia. It had been so long since she had had food she could no longer eat or drink on her own. The foot had been slashed by a rusty wire, and there was damage to the liver. The vet determined that the missing feathers had not been plucked out by another bird but yanked out by human hands. There were spots where the bird had been burned by cigarettes. The list of abuses went on and on. The vet provided antibiotics and instructions but made it clear the bird most likely would not survive. LC took her home, determined to prove the veterinarian wrong. She named the bird Patches.

The account and picture made me sick, and I had to log off. What kind of people would do such things to such a small and helpless animal? A bird, for god's sake, maybe still a baby. I tried to put it out of my mind, but I couldn't. I picked up Sugar Franklin and held her close to me for a long time, gently stroking her crest feathers the way she liked. If anyone ever hurt one of my birds I'd probably have to . . . well, I just couldn't think about it.

"Do you know how lucky you are," I whispered to Sugar. "Not every bird is as lucky as you."

Sugar Franklin did not respond, just turned her head slightly to guide my fingers to a more pleasurable place.

I was so upset that later that night I Googled animal rights groups, looking for the most radical ones. Suddenly I understood perfectly well why some people consider bombing labs where animal testing is being undertaken justified or why some groups insist all animals be free, including pets. We do not take seriously accounts of animal cruelty or question what goes on in slaughterhouses; no one wants to know how that nice juicy steak came to be on our plate -- we just want it at a cheap price with a minimum of fuss. We don't want to think about how beautiful exotic parrots are trapped and brought into this country; we just want a cute little bird we can love and spoil, preferably one that will match the interior design. I could not pretend I was any better.

I understood that night that it sometimes takes drastic negative measures to bring about beneficial changes and that maybe that was exactly what was required to begin to stop animal cruelty in any of its forms. No, I did not make any donations to these groups or join their lists, but that night I completely understood why someone would.

South Africa is seven hours ahead of Kentucky, so there was no news from LC until later the next day. Dozens of people had written in response to LC's first post; everyone as horrified as I was. Were there no such things as humane societies in South Africa? Was this kind of thing common over there? Why wasn't this pet store put out of business?

When LC wrote again, she said Patches had survived another night. She was feeding the bird formula every hour, teaching her how to eat again. LC disinfected the foot every 30 minutes, and took the bird back to the vet for hydration injections and a nasal flush. Two of the vets at the clinic reminded her that the bird could not possibly survive, but if LC was willing to try they would, too. They gave her more medication to disperse in steam, which LC had already started.

The pet store was well known in town for neglecting its animals, she said, but nothing was ever done by the authorities. They did have a humane society in town, but it had no power.

When I finished reading I tried to imagine what it must be like where LC lived. All I knew about South Africa was a little about apartheid and Nelson Mandela. I then tried to imagine how much, so far, the vet care was costing LC. Avian veterinarian care is far more expensive than dog or cat care in the United States, so it was probably even more expensive there. Her bill would be at least three hundred dollars, I guessed, probably a lot more. I imagined it would run into the thousands by the time Patches completely recovered. If she did recover.

The least I could do was send her a few dollars via PayPal. LC had not asked or even hinted for money from the Tiel Talk board, but there was nothing else I could do to help. And I desperately wanted to help this little bird survive in any way I could. If it had been one of my birds I'd go bankrupt.

I logged into PayPal and sent a few dollars to LC's e-mail. PayPal didn't list rands as a currency option, so I just stayed with dollars. In a few minutes, I got a notice from PayPal that my payment was refused. I checked that I had typed in LC's e-mail address correctly and resent the money. Again it was refused.

AL wrote that she'd heard privately from several people expressing concern and wanting to help. I gathered their names and e-mail addresses and said I would be glad to coordinate things.

Someone wrote that they didn't think PayPal would send money to South Africa, an explanation I found ridiculous. PayPal was accepted around the world, wasn't it? Surely, money was money -- South Africa or not.

LC wrote to me and asked that if people were determined to make donations, that they make those donations to their local rescues. She said that the vet bills had been 229 rand so far, which was about $34. Here in the United States we could only dream of such cheap avian care! She also confirmed that PayPal would not send funds to South Africa; they would only send funds from South Africa.

While discussions and ideas about how to help Patches continued, on Saturday I saw a string of green poop hanging from Sugar Franklin's vent. That was definitely not normal, but I couldn't imagine what was wrong. I cleaned her off, getting bitten several times for my trouble, and called Pennyroyal. Dr. Lacki said it could just be a reaction to the lupron injection she'd recently had and the "trauma" of the vet visit. Just watch her, Dr. Lacki said, and try not to worry.

There were several agencies that claimed to transfer money to South Africa, but none of them were near LC's town or else they charged ridiculous fees. Finally we all agreed to use MoneyGram, which I had found at one of the Wal-Mart Neighborhood stores near me.

Bev volunteered to accept everyone's money via PayPal and then send a money gram for the full amount of nearly two hundred dollars to LC at her husband's bank. Bev told me later that the woman at the MoneyGram counter kept trying to dissuade her from sending money to South Africa. Did Bev know these people? Had someone asked her send them money? There were all sorts of scams out there, she told Bev, and she didn't want her to be another victim.

LC continued daily updates on Patches' condition. She was very grateful for the money, and I told her to use any extra to start her own humane bird store.

Sugar Franklin began a heavy molt about this time and was unusually cranky and quiet. On Thursday night, a week after her lupron injection, I noticed that she felt lighter than usual. I put her on the scales and was shocked to see her weight had dropped to 94 grams. Her normal weight was 102 grams. The loss of weight is often the first and only sign of problems.

She wouldn't even hiss at my toes, and she normally hated my toes beyond all reason. She was having polyuria (excessive urine), and I didn't like the green color of her poop.

I covered her cage but left a corner open so I could see her. She wouldn't perch at her usual spot; she just stayed in the front corner of the cage, near me, looking at me. I could almost hear her thoughts: "I don't feel so good."

Once I took her out and tried to get her to stay with me under a quilt where she would be warmer, but she fussed so I put her back in the cage.

I slept on the couch beside her all night, as if

that would make her feel better or something. Around 3 I woke up and she was the same, both feet on the cage bottom, puffy, eyes closed.

I sent an e-mail to my supervisor that I had a sick bird and would have to take a vacation day.

The clinic opened at 7:30 and I was there by 7:25. Dr. Z was out and Dr. Lacki wasn't due until 8. Christine wasn't due in until later that morning.

Dr. Lacki and a vet tech listened to my stumbling account of Sugar's behavior.

She did a quick examination. I told her that Sugar had always had lots of liquid in her droppings. She hadn't been eating anything she shouldn't have, hadn't hurt herself. Dr. Lacki flipped through Sugar's chart and noted she had been tested for her kidney function, with no abnormal findings.

"Let's keep her here and run some tests," Dr. Lacki said. She ran through the names of the tests, and I nodded. She said she'd call me as soon as she knew something. The tech picked up Sugar and held her out to me. "Wanna say goodbye?" she asked.

I was so numb I didn't realize what she was saying. Goodbye? Was she dying? "What?" I said.

"I'm taking her back now," the tech said. "Did you want to say goodbye?"

I nodded and scritched Sugar's little head. I watched the tech take Sugar away. Dr. Lacki told me not to worry.

"Go on to work," she said. "We'll call you the minute we know something."

"I'll be at home," I told her. "Please call as soon as you find out what's going on."

As I left I realized I'd been babbling and

repeating myself in the clinic.

What if she dies, I kept asking myself as I drove home. Trying to imagine a life without that little yellow bird was impossible. It hurt, deep in my solar plexus.

But I'm a realist, I reminded myself. She would die, if not now then later. I had to be prepared for that.

When I got home I tried to catch up on usual household things, but finally gave up. If she dies I'll have her cremated, I told myself.

For some reason I thought of that night five years earlier when I took my father to the VA Hospital, after friends had found him wandering in southeast Kentucky. The Alzheimer's was very advanced by then, and I knew once we reached the hospital he would not be leaving alive. Then I remembered taking my 92-year-old grandmother to the hospital that April morning fifteen years ago, backing out of the driveway and knowing she would never see her house again.

Would Sugar Franklin ever see her home again?

Around noon I called the clinic.

They had gavaged her (aka force fed) and she was eating and drinking a little on her own. Dr. Lacki said Sugar was nippy, which was a good sign. Dr. Lacki was going to do some blood work to check on Sugar's renal function, and she talked about keeping her overnight in the incubator where it would be warm. She also gave Sugar some antibiotics, just in case. My job now was to wait. So far, without X-rays, the bill was about $350.

I wrote all my parrot-loving friends for any

prayers or healing energy they could offer up. Christine sent me an e-mail that Sugar Franklin looked very cozy in the incubator, but that she wasn't the feisty Sugar we all knew and loved.

Bev sent me $30 via PayPal. I tried to return it, but she refused. She said she might need money for her birds one day. I had to stop and cry again.

I turned on the television and watched Maury and Jerry Springer in a blur.

When the phone rang around three, it was Dr. Lacki.

"I've got news," she said, "and none of it is good."

"OK," I said, trying to brace myself against whatever was coming.

She began talking about uric acid levels and renal function. Sugar Franklin's uric acid levels were over 50; normal was about 10 or 11. She was seriously ill, and I should be prepared for the worst. They wanted to keep her in the hospital, where she would be given fluids and nutrition and medication. I agreed to everything Dr. Lacki was telling me. Finally, I asked if it would be all right for me to see my bird later that afternoon.

"Absolutely," Dr. Lacki said. "Why don't you come over around 4? There are some things I want to go over with you, too."

"How did this happen," I asked.

"We don't know," she said, "but it's not that uncommon."

I hung up the phone and sat there for a long time. Renal failure. Her little kidneys were no longer working properly. She couldn't live if she was in renal failure.

Be prepared for the worst, Dr. Lacki had said. Sugar Franklin was dying. My little yellow bird was dying. I looked at her empty cage. It was simply inconceivable to think of that cage being empty forever.

To distract myself I got on the computer again and began looking at funeral jewelry, for something suitable to put her ashes in. Somehow staring at urns and necklaces and stone markers was better than thinking about the necessity for such items.

My little yellow bird was dying. I tried to imagine what she was doing at that very moment. Was she in pain? Was she huddled in the corner of the incubator, sleeping? What was a uric acid level and why was hers so high? Had I made some terrible mistake in feeding her? Did I not keep her cage clean enough? Had I been too remiss in cleaning her water bottles?

I remembered all the times she would hurry over to the salt shaker on the end table to lick the top, and how she would hiss and fuss when I pulled her away. I thought of her frequent visits to her water bottle. Had we missed something during all those annual well-bird visits and blood tests? Had she been sick for years and no one knew? Had I let her eat pizza and peanuts too many times?

I told Charli and the cockatiels about Sugar Franklin's condition, but they ignored me. I considered cleaning Sugar's cage, but I couldn't bear to go near it. She might never see it again, with that perch covered in purple vet tape and that small white dish of pellets and Nutriberries, that ragged toy hanging from the top.

My little yellow bird.

Chapter Thirteen

I drove back to the clinic to see her that afternoon. She chirped at me several times, but I could tell she didn't feel well. She still had that sick bird look about her, but she let me pet her. I offered her some bits of almond and millet I had brought from home, which she refused. I left them for her in case she got her appetite back.

Dr. Lacki went over the test results with me and explained that one of the dangers of such high uric acid levels was gout. Gout could get so painful Sugar wouldn't be able to walk. Sugar's condition would continue to worsen, unless there was a genetic component to it, in which case she could live for years

Euthanasia, I thought. I will have to have her euthanized at some point. I asked Dr. Lacki how I would know when it was time to let Sugar Franklin go. Would she go into convulsions or start falling over or what? Dr. Lacki said she wasn't going to let it get that bad. She promised she would tell me when it was time.

I managed to sleep a little that night. When I got up the next morning I uncovered the cockatiels, then uncovered Charli, then moved to uncover Sugar . . . but of course she wasn't there.

I watched the cockatiels for a few minutes, thinking about Sugar. There was a silly game she liked to play with me -- she would stand in the corner of her cage nearest me, watching. I would point my index finger at her and slowly move my finger closer and closer and closer -- she would hold perfectly still, watching, until my finger was about a quarter inch away from her little face. Then she would chirp loudly and fluff up, then hold very still and wait for me to do it again. Until she got bored with the game and would prance away in her little Queen Empress of the Universe walk.

Still thinking of Sugar I tried it with Nicholas. He just stared at me with his "look, the idiot human is acting weird again" look. I realized it would be so easy to see my other birds through the Sugar Franklin lens, which would be terribly unfair to them.

I made some french toast for myself and the birds. The tech called while we were eating and said Sugar was continuing to lose weight, but she was very feisty and seemed to have eaten most of a Nutriberri, which warmed my heart.

I tried to imagine what it would be like without Sugar Franklin. Things would probably be a little more simple for everyone. The cockatiels wouldn't have to share a travel cage, and there would be a big open space left by the window when I was finally emotionally able to put away her cage. The Nutriberries and seed bar treats would go farther. Cleaning cages and changing out all the toys would take less time. I would learn to schedule and divide things by three instead of four.

I began to cry again.

Christine and Bev suggested we get together for lunch at our favorite pizza place that Saturday, and I was happy to agree. I knew they cared about both me and Sugar Franklin and would listen to me talk about Sugar for hours if that was what I needed, but it felt better to talk about mundane things.

I cried so much over the weekend that I now had peeling skin on the tip and sides of my nose. I had to constantly check this when I left the house lest it appear to others that I was walking around with snot smeared all over me. Not that I cared what anyone thought.

Dr. Lacki called when I returned home and persuaded me to go see Sugar Franklin on Sunday. I told her I was reluctant to disturb her for my benefit, and she said Sugar would most likely benefit a lot more from being with me. That had never occurred to me, and I felt even more selfish.

Dr. Lacki said her scientific side wanted to keep Sugar at the clinic until Monday, but her sympathetic side told her that Sugar might be feel better being at home around familiar surroundings instead of being around strange people who kept poking her with things. She repeated that it would be all right if I decided to take her home.

Did I dare bring her home? On the one hand I wanted her to be as stuffed with healing medications and nutrients and fluids as possible. On the other hand, I missed her so much. I thought the other birds did, too. They kept going over to her closed cage and wanting in so they could eat her food. I decided that might be the highest form of honor a cockatiel could give to another cockatiel.

I placed several small shallow bowls of water in her cage and moved the perches so she wouldn't have to climb more than necessary. I put bits of millet stalks in her food dishes and on the grate of the cage. She would have to expend very little energy to eat or drink.

Before I left for the clinic, I ordered an Avi-Tech AviTemp from the manufacturer's website. An AviTemp was a small box that emits heat at a low and steady temperature, designed to hang outside the cage. It would take care of the problem of how to keep Sugar Franklin warm. That left me with about $20 until pay day, but I didn't care.

Around five o'clock I gathered up Sugar's travel cage and went to the clinic. "Dr. Lacki said it would be okay to take her home," I told the two techs, "but I want to see how she's doing." The first tech nodded and went to get Sugar Franklin.

When she came back she was carrying a large bundle of white towel in her cupped hands. The tips of two impertinent yellow crest feathers were sticking out. I knew then I had to have her home with me.

The tech handed the bundle to me and I unwrapped it. Sugar politely stepped onto my finger. Her weight felt good, her feathers looked good, she looked healthy and wonderful. Had she really been sick?

I put her on my shoulder. I leaned my cheek against her warm feathers.

The techs answered my questions, instructed me on how to give the assortment of medications, reminded me how important it was to get her to drink as much water as possible, and so on. They explained that heat would help the gout in her feet and that the gout might mean she wouldn't perch or climb as easily. Sugar sat on my shoulder through the whole thing, pooping on me once. She wouldn't let me scritch her. I kept my cheek against her soft feathers, probably drawing more strength from her than I gave. She looked so much better than I had dared hope; a thousand times better than she had on Friday.

The second tech suggested socks of hot rice to help keep the cage warm. I had no rice in the house, and she offered to stop by a grocery and pick some up for me.

Since all of the charges were being put on a special credit card for veterinarian bills, I didn't have to come up with any cash before I took Sugar Franklin home. The terms of the credit card would allow me to take up to a year to pay without interest; I knew I'd probably need more than a year to pay it off.

When Sugar Franklin saw her travel cage she flapped her wings for a minute, then went inside without a fuss. We went outside. I stood with her for a few minutes in the sunlight. She listened intently to the wild birds chirping and, I hoped, soaked in some of the sun's warmth.

During the drive home she kept her back to me, staring at the door or at the scenes flashing by the window.

"Don't you want to talk to me?" I asked her back feathers. I received silence in return. "Well, I don't care how mad you are at me. We're going home."

When I pulled the car into the driveway, I said, "We're home, sweetie!" I picked up her cage and walked to the front door. For the first time, she chirped.

When we walked into the front hall she chirped again, and all the birds chirped back before we even reached the living room. I held the cage up to everyone and there was a great rejoicing of chirps (except from Charli, who seemed to view this new development with disdain). This went on for a few minutes, and I began to cry again, only this time with happiness.

I took Sugar out of her travel cage. I wanted to hold her and pet her for a moment, but she leaned toward her cage. So I gently put her in, and she immediately went to her cloth perch, to the highest point, and began preening.

The cockatiels clung to the side of their cage closest to Sugar's and watched her for a long time. Once she walked to the side of the cage and climbed up to survey the room, then went back to the perch high up and returned to preening. Except for the new position of items in her cage it was as if she'd never been gone.

The tech brought me a bag of white rice to put in socks and microwave for heat. I showed her Sugar up on her perch and she said that was a good sign, that bringing Sugar home had clearly been the right thing to do. She gave me some tips about keeping Sugar warm, and agreed that one of the cockatiel's heated perches would be great for her little feet. Before she left she repeated that I was to call the emergency number if something changed.

I explained to Nicholas and Flash that I was taking one of their heated perches to give to Sugar but that it wouldn't be forever and that if they tried to at least make an effort they could share the remaining one. They didn't seem impressed. They watched me untangle the cords and install one of the perches in Sugar's cage.

She didn't grip any of her perches very tightly, but that was the only thing I could see that was different. Sugar didn't seem to have any problem with climbing. She watched me make the heated perch fit into her cage, and then ignored it. as she had when I had first bought them months ago.

She had a bowl full of millet and Nutriberries at her disposal. I would leave a bowl of infant bird formula for her in the morning, and determined I would weigh the bowls when I got home from work so I could tell if she'd eaten. I taped a sheet of paper on the wall above the scale so I could easily write in numbers and dates.

My baby was home! I began to cry again. She could ignore me and be as mad at me as she wanted; I didn't care. She was home.

Chapter Fourteen

I awoke early the next morning. I would begin giving Sugar Franklin her medications, and I worried it would take a long time.

I filled a syringe with the three medications. Dr. Lacki said two of them would help with some of the calcification from the gout. She had told me I didn't have to worry about the left side or right side; to just get the medications into her mouth and Sugar would take care of the rest.

I picked up Sugar and held her head with my left hand and pressed the syringe against the right side of her beak with my right hand. She clamped her beak shut and squirmed. I gently pried open her beak with my left thumb just enough to get the very tip of the syringe into her mouth. I slowly, slowly pressed the plunger.

Sugar Franklin fought and squirmed so hard that most of the meds ended up on her beak and feathers. I put her back in her cage, where she climbed onto the perch and wiped her beak on it. She turned her back to me. We would have more time that evening, I told myself. She would get used to it. It would be easier next time.

Sugar was on the highest perch when I got home from work. She didn't seem all that impressed to see me, and I missed seeing her running back and forth, back and forth with excitement when I came in.

By the pile of poop I could tell she'd stayed on her perch all day. Dark green poop, some urates, and of course urine.

She was most definitely not interested in coming out of the cage or having my hand in the cage when it was time for evening's meds. I cut up some fresh grapes and watermelon, and then offered her the bowl. Nope. Sugar generally loved grapes, so I was disappointed when she turned her beak up at them. I sat there for a while, with the cage door open, admiring her. I picked up and ate a couple of pieces of watermelon from her bowl; she watched but wasn't fooled. I then just looked at her for a while again. She seemed a bit more bright-eyed than she had when I'd left for work. Unless I was imagining it.

She then decided to climb down from her perch; it was hard for her. She came to the door of the cage and then gracefully stepped up on my finger. And allowed me to scritch her little head. Which I did for about fifteen minutes. I hoped she'd forgiven me or at least put me on probation.

After scritches she climbed onto my shoulder and we went to the kitchen. I prepared the meds. Dr. Lacki had given me a narcotic med to help with any pain Sugar Franklin was having.

Sugar Franklin watched all of this with great interest, occasionally chirping to encourage me along. Perhaps she thought I was preparing the syringe for myself. I wrapped her up in a towel and so we began again.

Most of the time I ended up squirting the meds onto the side of her tongue, one drop at a time. Then I would stop and scritch her little head. Then start again. Soon her head would become coated with the medications that smeared onto my fingers.

It was frightening how tiny her head was in my fingers. I could have crushed it like an egg. She glared at me with her red eyes, kicked her little feet, and squirmed and fought until the towel would come loose. I would have to put down the syringe and wrap her again in the towel, then hold her by the neck, pick up the syringe, and start again.

The clear narcotic was given in such a tiny amount I worried I hadn't given her enough or that it all hadn't come out of the syringe when I filled up the extra syringe with the other meds. When I was done with the meds I pulled in some water into the syringe and gave her that, too.

It took nearly an hour.

Back in the kitchen she watched me rinse out the syringes and put the meds back in the fridge. Dr. Lacki had suggested I try giving Sugar Franklin Pedialyte to help her fluid intake. I poured some in a bowl -- which Sugar refused. I dipped my finger in it and offered her my finger. Nope. I licked my finger and made yummy sounds. Nope.

She preened for a while and then took a nap.

I called my piano teacher, and told her I'd have to miss my lesson the next day and that I hadn't even considered practicing over the weekend.

I searched the freezer to see if the Ice Cream Fairy had deposited some Haagan-Daz or any kind of ice cream in there but was disappointed to find only frozen vegetables and birdie bread.

I soon developed a dismal routine for evenings and mornings. Medication administration and begging forgiveness took over 30 minutes. Cleaning out syringes took a few minutes.

Periodically washing out food dishes so I'd have plenty on hand took a while.

Preparing watery fruits and then attempting to get Sugar to eat some took more time. Playing with the other birds and reassuring them that I didn't love Sugar more than I loved them took time. Offering, begging, and threatening Sugar to take in more fluids took a longer time. Changing Sugar's cage papers and weighing food took a few minutes. Fixing dinner took a while.

Mixing meds for the morning took forever -- a couple of times I accidently mixed up one of the medications with the narcotic, have to toss that out, drop a note to Dr. Lacki that I might run short on meds because of my mistake, start all over with the meds, clean out syringes, wash a few more food dishes. I covered up all the birds past their bed time, taking more time to heat rice-filled socks and arrange things in Sugar's cage.

By the time I was finished it was usually well after 9:30. In a kind of stupor, I would sit on the couch and stared at the television for a while. Then realize I hadn't given Nicholas any scritches. Bad bird mommy.

I was too pathetic to even think about.

I wrote daily updates to Bev and Christine and other friends both in real life or on the Tiel Talk board. Their encouraging responses and suggestions never failed to make me feel better.

The following week I took Sugar Franklin back to the vet for blood work and some hydration. She was alert during the ride to the vet's. I usually had the car radio set to NPR or a rock and roll station, but this time I switched to a jazz station for a change. Sugar perked up and watched the radio with interest. She chirped happily. She liked jazz! She had never shown any preferences for music or television, but she was definitely responding to the jazz.

I was willing to beg piously for the vet techs to give Sugar her meds, so they were kind enough to gavage her with formula and two of the meds. Dr. Lacki was pleased Sugar was perching and started calling her the "miracle bird." But Sugar's weight was 90 grams -- 11 grams too light. Dr. Lacki gave me some suggestions to try and get Sugar to eat more.

On the way home I played more jazz for her, which she seemed to enjoy.

Back at home I let her alone, let her sleep. I imagined drawing blood from her tiny, tiny body and the stress of the vet visit had worn her out.

The AviTemp finally arrived, and I was so happy to be rid of the routine of heating rice-filled socks and arranging them in the cage.

I decided that I'd been pushing too hard; pushing food and water on her, asking her to eat this, drink that, try that, is she asleep, is she awake, where is she on the perch, and so on. I figured we needed some quality quiet time together, with no orders or expectations.

I put her on the couch and she climbed up to the back of it to preen. I turned the old halogen lamp on very low. She stayed under that for 15 minutes or so, getting her feathers all nice and straight. When she had finished preening, she just stood there, studying me with that little face of hers. Finally I picked her up and spent a long time petting her.

Dr. Z called with the lab results. Sugar's uric acid had been over 50 the previous Friday. Now it was 26 something, which was still way above normal but so much better. Dr. Z said this indicated the amount of kidney failure, and calculated that Sugar had lost about 16 percent. Her phosphorus had been high and now it was well within the normal range. She said that if the phosphorus levels didn't go down none of the other levels would matter.

Dr. Z said she was very cautiously optimistic, and I decided to allow myself to be, too. The mysterious news about Dr. Z had finally become public; she had accepted a position with Iowa State University and the sale of Pennyroyal to a local vet was imminent. Even though Dr. Lacki was treating Sugar Franklin it was always in the back of my mind that Dr. Z, with decades more experience and knowledge, was available to step in at a moment's notice. Now that she was leaving what would I do if Sugar required an advanced expert diagnosis or procedure?

Sugar Franklin was always much better after her bi-weekly trip to the clinic for gavage and hydration; I wondered about learning to do that at home. Dr. Z reassured me that I could learn and that the percentages were very good I wouldn't aspirate her. I said I'd think about it. I was still terrified I'd aspirate her and kill her, just as I thought I had so long ago. Plus gavage required two people.

I asked Bev and Christine if they would

consider coming to my house every few days or so to hold Sugar for me while I did the gavage. They both immediately responded that they would be glad to help.

In the midst of vet visits and medication fights and worry sessions, I received word that my book of poems was finally going to be published. The news made me happy, of course, but I knew I'd give up the book in a heartbeat to save Sugar Franklin.

Christine was suddenly wooed away from Pennyroyal by a dog and cat veterinary hospital, just before the sale of Pennyroyal was announced. Though she would miss the bird clients, she was happy she wouldn't have to risk being laid off.

On some days I was angry with Sugar Franklin for making things so difficult, and angry with veterinary medicine in general that it couldn't fix things. I got angry at having to miss my piano lessons, angry at the mounting bills from Pennyroyal, and angry that I'd been foolish enough to get a parrot as a pet rather than a dog or cat like a normal person would.

I accused Sugar of not being all that sick, that she was just pretending in order to get unlimited treats and attention. No matter how pitiful she acted or what kind of fuss she put up or how decimated she looked, she didn't fool me a bit, I told her. She would take her meds and formula and like it. I reminded her that I could be a pretty good drama queen myself.

Other days I tried to work with Sugar Franklin as if she belonged to a client, using every aspect of positive reinforcement I could think up. I kept special treats at hand, was always providing extra scritches. I chatted casually with her, explaining what was in the syringe and what the next step in the process would be.

At times I lectured her, explaining that if she really wanted to get well she had to eat and drink. There was no way around it, I would explain patiently. I was trying to help her, but she had to want to get well, and she had best come around soon. If she wanted to die she was going to have to do it on her own time, that I wasn't having it. Sometimes it seemed to me that she "got" it, that she understood I was trying to help her, but she continued to fight.

Nothing was easy or quick.

Chapter Fifteen

The syringes were getting worn and loose. I told myself to ask Christine for some extras. I picked up a clean one to see what size it was. It held a total of one cc.

It came to me suddenly that I'd been making a horrible mistake. I stood there, stunned. A sense of horror washed through me. What had I done? I'd been giving Sugar Franklin the correct amount of medications -- baytril 0.04; allupuril 0.04; clochiline 0.4. But when it came to the formula/pedialyte/water mixture I had only been pulling 0.8cc, not the prescribed 8.0cc.

The tech told me that they had given her 4.0cc of formula, and I had been so proud I'd gotten what I was thinking was 5-7.0ccs down her, when in reality it was less than one cc. No wonder Sugar was always so much improved after Pennyroyal -- she was getting a lot of formula and fluids. I had been giving her teeny amounts. No wonder her weight was dropping.

I couldn't believe I'd been running around, doing all this and still letting her slowly starve! Since she didn't feel good she was only eating three to five grams a day on her own; it was the formula in full ccs from Pennyroyal that had been helping so much. There must be a parrot god up there somewhere, protecting her from me, the one human who cared more for her than anyone else in the world.

That night I managed to get at least 3 full ccs of her formula mixture down her plus her meds. She ate some millet and took a drink of water after her traumatic ordeal, then settled in to sleep.

For myself, I seriously considered the bottle of whiskey in the kitchen to settle my nerves, but I knew it would take more than a quart to do it.

I wrote to Christine, confessing my error. She told me that she had done the same sort of things, that I was a fallible human being and should not beat myself up over it. The important thing was that I caught the error and wouldn't make the same mistake again.

She wrote, "I have to say, though, sitting in my chair, I think you've done a wonderful job with Sugar. I've seen birds at Pennyroyal who died from a lifetime of neglect (and so have you!), a few from abuse or willful ignorance, and an awful lot from downright accidents, from the bird who was run over with a power chair and partially skinned alive, to the one who ate every meal with the family dog until the one day the dog decided he didn't want to share anymore ...

"We both know Sugar would have been gone a long time ago without your love and care, so I hope you're not forgetting that, plus the fact that the parrot god was clearly looking out for her in that comment about the ccs. See? He really does work in mysterious ways!"

While I appreciated and needed to hear Christine's reassurances I still felt uneasy when people pointed out that I was taking extraordinary care of Sugar Franklin. She was my responsibility; why would I not take care of her? Intellectually I knew plenty of people would just let her die, but I couldn't imagine myself sitting around doing nothing to help her feel better. I loved her; I wanted her to be healthy and happy. Of course I would do everything I could for her.

The next morning I forced about 1.5 full ccs down her, plus her meds. In between doses, I would gently pet her head and tell her what a good bird she was. This never seemed to impress her enough to hold still though.

While the medication was dribbling down into her face feathers, she would clamp her beak shut so the remaining medications squished out the sides of her beak, too.

I would wipe her face with a wet tissue and start again. For all the good I was doing I may as well just have squirted the medication onto the tissue and been done with it.

Sugar Franklin would bite down on the syringe, but only so she could stick her tongue on the end of it so I wouldn't be able to press the plunger. Should I manage to get the syringe past her tongue and squirt a drop or two into the side of her mouth, she would let it all dribble down the sides of her beak. Then look up at me as if to say, "I may look pitiful, but you are an idiot."

Once in a great while I would get a drop or two under her tongue. This infuriated her so much she would kick even harder and shake her head and act as if she'd been poisoned. She then would glare at me, promising to get even as soon as she got out of that towel.

While all this was going on she would secretly be slowly loosening the towel under my fingers so that when I attempted to give her another drop of medication she would suddenly flap her wings loose and the towel would fall to my lap. Lucky for me I usually still had a reasonable grip on her neck; otherwise, she'd be over on the other side of the room.

I would drape the towel over her and start again.

She bit my thumb so often and so hard during these rounds that I began to develop skin tags on my thumb from her beak.

When we were finally finished with the syringe and I let her out of the towel, she would either hop onto the back of the couch to be under the halogen light or just stand still and glare at me for a few seconds. Then she would turn her back to me and go off to her cage to sulk.

The other birds were silent during these feeding times -- they stood and watched. There was no way to know for sure what they thought about the situation. Were they wondering if I was planning to torture them, too?

I kept thinking if I could get her over this, could get her weight up and have her drinking more water, she would be back to as close to normal as she would ever be. I knew the damage done to her kidneys would never heal. Then I would wonder if I was doing her any good or just wearing her out. Or was this now her new "normal," and we would have to do the meds/formula fight twice a day until one of us died?

Her weight hovered around 87 or 89, which bothered me. Dr. Lacki said that wasn't a big issue, that her weight would fluctuate, and the important thing was that she was alive and stable.

My other three parrots were so healthy and happy. Why couldn't Sugar Franklin be healthy and happy, too?

Chapter Sixteen

The church was dark and cool inside, with only the light over the piano's keyboard shining. Oxana, the woman who was teaching me piano, smiled when she saw me. I put a towel on the front pew and put Sugar Franklin's cage on the towel.

"Thank you for this," I said. "She's spent so much time at the vet's I wanted to give her a change of scenery. I wanted her to know that a trip in the car doesn't always end up at the clinic."

Oxana came over and smiled Sugar. "She is beautiful!" she exclaimed. "She doesn't look sick at all." Sugar stared up at Oxana, then at me.

I nodded. "I know. Birds hide their illness."

I sat down at the piano and opened my music book. It had been over a month, and I hadn't practiced much. I tentatively pressed the keys, picking out the song in the beginner's music book.

"Good," Oxana said. "Now, again."

Whenever I glanced at Sugar Franklin, she was transfixed, as silent as the proverbial church mouse. She did not even offer any criticism of my playing as she usually did when I practiced at home.

After the lesson I put Sugar Franklin back in the car. She fluffed up with pleasure and chirped several times. I was grateful she had enjoyed the concert. During the ride home she climbed to the top of the cage to better see the scenery pass by. I turned the radio on to the jazz station.

The next morning she again fought cleverly when it came time for meds and formula. Somehow a spot on her right wing was bleeding; had I been too rough with the towel? Or was she so thin now that her skin was paper? My heart sank.

My little yellow bird.

As I watched her I wondered if I shouldn't just let her go, start weaning myself of hope and determination. If she was just going to wither away why not let her go? What kind of life was it for her, being force-fed meds and formula twice a day, and staying in the warmest spot in the cage, next to the AviTemp?

Because of the upcoming Fourth of July holiday Pennyroyal would be closed on Monday, so I took her on Friday for hydration. She had been scheduled to have blood work done the following week, but we decided to do that on Friday as well.

The blood work, about a month after the initial diagnosis, would give us a better idea of what to do, what to expect, how much more medication, and so on.

It had felt like six months to me, not four weeks.

When the results were ready, Dr. Lacki came out with Sugar's file in her hand. She pointed to a piece of paper and said, "They all came back normal."

I stood there with my mouth open.

"Normal?"

Dr. Lacki nodded and showed me a row of numbers, which meant absolutely nothing to me.

Normal?

"Are you sure you've got the right bird?"

Dr. Lacki said she was going to check with Dr. Z, but as far as she was concerned I could drop the morning meds and just do meds at night. She reminded me to watch Sugar's weight.

Sugar's weight was still 87, and I remembered that Nicholas weighed something like 65 or 68 and shouldn't have been living at all, yet he was the noisiest full-of-himself bird I had. So if Sugar wanted to weigh 87, that was just fine with me.

Sugar Franklin continued to improve through the summer. Work remained as political and disheartening as ever, and I continued to scour the university's listing of job openings and the want ads. Conversations and e-mails slowly turned to other, happier topics than Sugar Franklin's illness.

When I took Sugar Franklin for a follow-up visit a few months later Dr. Lacki was thrilled. She said Sugar Franklin looked wonderful, her weight was wonderful, her body mass felt good, her feet were in good shape -- everything seemed wonderful. We could stop the medications all together.

I thought we might have some blood work done, but Dr. Lacki said she'd rather wait until at least two months since the last time I gave Sugar meds, so I agreed to wait.

Dr. Lacki kept saying, "This is a miracle bird," and that I had a whole lot to do with Sugar's recovery. I told her that she and the staff also had a lot to do with it. Plus all my friends (face-to-face and electronic), since they had all held my hand through the summer.

Little Miss Miracle Bird had a fine dinner of pasta, Harrison's pellets, and some Nutriberries that evening. Then took a well-deserved nap.

For the first time since late May Sugar fussed

and yelled at my bare toes. She did not appear to be aware of how sick she was or what we had gone through helping her get better -- the ungrateful little diva -- but I was joyous to hear her indignant vocalizations about my naked toes. She even played the index finger game with me several times.

She frequently stood in front of the AviTemp, staring at it. I wasn't sure if this was because of its warmth or if she was trying to figure out what had happened to the scene she was used to seeing out that side of her cage. She was so cute when she sat there studying on the matter, her head tilted slightly to the side.

She began masturbating again and doing the skirt dance, which meant she was in the mood to lay some eggs. After running up a bill of $1,112.67 getting her well from renal failure I most certainly did not want her laying so many eggs she might get egg bound.

Chapter Seventeen

Sugar Franklin's weight was high two nights before her next appointment. When I got home from work on Thursday, the day before her appointment, Sugar had laid an egg, and her weight was down again. I gave her a strong lecture about the dangers of laying eggs, which she listened to as well as anything else I said.

On the drive to Pennyroyal I promised Sugar I wouldn't leave her there again. I explained that she would be staying for the day to be hydrated and watched while I was at work. She chirped once in agreement and went back to her preening.

Dr. Lacki called me at work with the results; normal uric acid levels were 10; hers were 21. She said I'd have to put Sugar Franklin back on her meds and that the clinic had called in the prescription for fresh medications at a local compounding drug store.

After work I picked up the drugs, then picked up Sugar Franklin. Dr. Lacki pointed out the bald spot on Sugar's head, which seemed redder than usual. She said Sugar had a bad hematoma just below where she was stuck with the needle and told me to keep an eye on it.

During the drive home I saw a gray streak on either side of Sugar Franklin's beak, which I thought was probably dust. She gorged herself on millet and took several drinks of water. She was perky and full of herself; perfectly normal.

When we got home it seemed the streaks on her beak were more pronounced. I wet my finger and rubbed one side of her beak; it wasn't dust or dirt. The bald spot on her head was very red and blotted, as if she were bleeding under her skin.

I put Sugar in her cage, where she began the never-ending task of preening. I sorted through the bills and threw out the junk mail. When I looked at Sugar again one of her nares (nostrils) was very dark. I looked closer. It was blood.

I called Pennyroyal and said I was on my way back. Sugar began bleeding from both nares, but it wasn't oozing out or actively running down her beak, just both nares with big spots of blood.

My heart was pounding as I put her back in her travel cage. Was she bleeding to death? She seemed so calm and unaffected by what was happening. I kept telling myself not to panic, to be calm, to focus on getting back to the clinic.

The techs were waiting for me and led me into the surgery room as soon as I arrived. Dr. Lacki examined Sugar but had no idea what was going on. She put Sugar Franklin in an oxygen chamber for the night. She said in some cases such bleeding could be liver damage, but it those cases the bleeding was widespread, not just localized in one part of the body. She said that, for example, Sugar's feet were a perfect color. Dr. Lacki said it was highly unlikely to be liver damage since she was acting so normal in all the important ways. There was no blood anywhere else.

I spent a few minutes in the surgery room with Sugar Franklin. She was in the oxygen chamber, looking at me through the little window in its door. She was not happy, and the dark spot at her nare made her look even angrier. I apologized for having to leave her there after promising I wouldn't. She turned her back to me. It was for her own good, I told her. She shouldn't be bleeding like that. Even if she never looked at me again, I said, I still loved her and would be back first thing in the morning.

When I got home I explained to the other birds what was going on, but as usual they gave no indication they understood, though I suspected they had lengthy discussions about Sugar Franklin when we weren't home. I opened the cages so they could come out if they wanted, and began changing the paper in Sugar's cage.

The next morning when I arrived at the clinic Sugar Franklin was perky, eating and drinking and pooping and acting perfectly normal. There had been no more bleeding.

Dr. Lacki and the other vets had done more research the night before and had found only two instances of this particular incident. She explained that when they had taken blood the previous day they might have slightly nicked one of the tiny air sacs behind the vein. If so, blood may have seeped into the air sac and then circulated through Sugar Franklin's head and beak. Evidently, this little air sac only circulates through the head cavity, which would explain why she wasn't bleeding anywhere else.

They told me that this happens frequently, especially with little birds, but normally the nicks close back up almost immediately. The two instances they turned up during their research were like Sugar -- bleeding through the nares.

The prognosis was that it would clear up but would take a while. Dr. Lacki said to bring her back on Tuesday. In the meantime I was to try to keep Sugar Franklin calm and relaxed; I could skip trying to force the medications down her beak for the next few days.

When we got home Sugar Franklin settled down in her cage, sitting in her food dish as she always did when she was expecting an egg. I wanted to shake her little yellow feathers -- how could she be thinking of eggs after the past two days?

I was not upset or angry with Dr. Lacki. I'd seen how hard it is to do blood draws on a cranky, fussy, twisting little bird and was always amazed they got any at all. I was relieved Sugar was going to be all right, and even happier I didn't have to give her medications.

I took a couple of pictures of Sugar's nares and then tried to get caught up with my e-mail. LC in South Africa reported that Patches was doing well. "She comes out of her cage on her own, and even enjoys a misting now and then." Someone on Tiel Talk announced that their cockatiel had laid an egg, too.

Sugar Franklin's beak stayed blue-gray throughout the weekend, but she chirped happily and demanded scritches most of the time. Which I was happy to provide.

On Sunday morning, late September now, I sat and watched Sugar Franklin run back and forth, back and forth, in her cage at approximately 70 miles an hour, wanting out. I took her out and put her on my shoulder, where she helpfully chirped directly into my ear. She occasionally stretched out, first one wing and then the other. Her weight on my shoulder felt normal and solid. Sometimes she faced forward to chirp at the other birds, then she would turn around and chirp at the couch.

It had been so long since she had been this happy and active and vocal -- no one would guess how sick she had been. I felt so grateful to the vets, the techs, my friends, and the great parrot spirit that she was still here to poop on my shoulder and chirp in my ear.

I got out the big bag of Nutriberries. She had certainly earned some extra treats.

Chapter Eighteen

The following Monday I was late getting home. I had to stop at the grocery. I was nearly out of gas and had to stop to fill up. When I opened the gas cap I noticed a scratch and a small dent – as if someone had tried to pry the door open. My heart sank. I should probably call the police when I got home.

When I came in to the house none of the birds chirped their usual greeting to me. I looked at Sugar Franklin. She was on the lowest part of the perch, eyes closed, barely able to stand.

"Oh baby," I whispered.

I took her out of the cage and tried to hold her. One of her wings flapped open, loose, as if she couldn't hold it in its normal position. Her weight was 95, down from 107 yesterday. Her entire body was limp.

I tried to hold her, but she insisted on climbing onto my shoulder and staring at the wall.

I called Pennyroyal. The tech who answered and said that neither Dr. Lacki or Dr. Garrison were in. "She'll be here in the morning."

"She won't live that long," I said.

"You want me to call Dr. Lacki and have her call you?"

"Yes, please." I put down the phone and took Sugar off my shoulder.

"Oh baby." I held her lightly against my heart and stroked her head. "If you need to go, you go, okay? Don't you stay for me, sweetie." I whispered. "Thank you for waiting for me to get home." Tears spilled down my cheeks.

I had noticed the day before that she had been more quiet than usual, but sometimes she was that way just before she laid an egg so I hadn't thought too much about it. I felt stupid for not paying closer attention.

I got up and took her to the door to look out at the yard for a moment. Then I took her to Charli's cage, who ignored her. I showed her the cockatiels, who chirped a little. I took her into the study and talked about that day I spent feeding her bits of peanuts, about how she had flung the water bottle cap at me that day in the study, how she used to climb the lace curtains to the top where I couldn't reach her. I reminded her of all the new and wonderful things she had taught me, all the new friends I'd made because of her.

I went back to the living room and sat by the phone. I continued to stroke her head and rocked a little. "Thank you," I whispered to her. "You changed my life, all for the better. If you need to go, sweetheart, it's okay. Please don't stay for me." I had to whisper because I knew my voice would break if I tried to speak normally.

She was so light in my hands it felt as if I were holding a down feather.

The phone rang. I described Sugar's condition to Dr. Lacki.

"Bring her in," she said.

I interrupted her. "She may not live that long. I don't know what to do. Should I just let her die at home?"

"She could be egg bound," Dr. Lacki said. "We can do a lot for her."

Egg bound? I gently lifted Sugar up. Her vent looked normal. If she were egg bound, wouldn't her vent be a tiny bit swollen?

"Go ahead and get her to the clinic," Dr. Lacki repeated. "I'll call and tell them to get ready for her. We'll get her in the incubator and get some fluids in her."

I knew she wasn't egg bound but what if I was wrong and there was something they could do for her?

"Ok," I said. "Would you please call and tell them I'm coming?"

"Yes. Go ahead and bring her in. They'll be ready for her."

I gently put Sugar Franklin in her little travel cage and ran out to the car. It was after five and I knew traffic would be miserable, but I also knew I had to keep calm because every moment counted now. Maybe, maybe, maybe.

The receptionist immediately waved me on into the surgery room, past the clients with their dogs in the waiting room. The two techs had the scales ready, a big clear bowl setting on top. As gently and tenderly as I could I took Sugar out of the cage while one of the techs held the cage door open for me. I put her in the bowl.

The tech noted her weight – 95. "Poop?" she asked the other tech.

We all looked at the cage papers. Nothing. The techs exchanged the briefest, barest of looks, which I knew I wasn't meant to see.

Sugar looked up at me while the first tech wrote things in the chart. Her eyes were round and dark. She was bewildered but far too sick to protest. I gently petted her soft little head and took a step backward.

"What do I do now," I asked. "Should I stay?"

"We're going to medicate her and get some fluids in her. You can stay if you want." the tech said. I scritched Sugar Franklin's head again, softly.

"Call me," I said. I knew there was nothing I could do and that I would only be in the way. I got back in the car and cried all the way home.

I was so tired. When I got home I sat on the couch and cried, staring at her empty cage.

I sent an e-mail to Bev and Christine. Christine called and we talked a little while. I kept saying that I hoped Sugar would die because she couldn't keep going on this way, her kidneys failing, her weight up and down, the upcoming battles with the medications. It would be a blessing, I said, if she just died. But I didn't want her to die. I wanted her home, well and whole. I wanted my Sugar Franklin.

I wanted her to be egg bound and for the techs to call and say an egg had passed successfully and all was well.

The next morning I stood beside the phone for a few minutes until about 7:35. The clinic opened at 7:30, but the techs arrived around 7. If Sugar Franklin had died in the night they would have called me.

The phone remained silent so I knew she'd survived the night.

I drove directly to the clinic. As I got out of my car I saw the receptionist leave the front desk and disappear into the lab area. I went in and waited for her to return. It seemed she was gone a long time. I glanced through the big plate glass window. How bright the sun was that morning. I had slept badly the night before.

The lab door opened and the receptionist came out with the tech. The tech put her hand on my shoulder, "I'm so sorry," she said.

I looked at her face then at the receptionist.

"Did she die?" I said. "I was hoping she'd die," I heard myself say.

"I'm so sorry, Marguerite. She was gone when we got here this morning."

I nodded. "I was hoping she'd die," I repeated.

"I'm sorry," the receptionist said.

The tech asked if I wanted to see her. I nodded. She led me to an exam room and left. In a few minutes she came in, holding a bundle in a white towel as if she were holding a baby. This time there were no little crest feathers showing over the towel.

I took the bundle from her and unwrapped it.

"You take your time," the tech said as she left the room.

"Oh Sugar," I whispered. "Oh baby." Her body was warm from the incubator and there was still dried blood on her nare. I stroked her soft, soft feathers, from her head, down her back. Her feet, always curled a bit, were now straight and seemed oddly large. Had her feet always been that big?

I took a deep breath and realized I'd stopped breathing. I pressed her small body against my face, wetting her feathers with my tears. "Thank you," I whispered to her, "for everything. I am so sorry," over and over.

There was nothing else to say, nothing else to do. She was dead. Gone. All that wonderful energy and life and noise was gone, never to return.

I took another breath and slowly wrapped her back in the towel.

I took her back to the lobby and handed her to the tech. "I'd like her cremated, please," I said. The thought of having a necropsy done crossed my mind, but what was the point?

"Are you okay?" I heard someone ask. I nodded and went out to the car.

Her cage. Her little travel cage was still inside the clinic. I went back inside and the tech had it in her hand. I took the cage, and drove home. I cried all the way home, as I had before. I didn't care if people in surrounding cars saw me crying. They were speeding to jobs and schools; I had just lost one of the most important things in my life.

"My baby is gone. Gone," kept running through my head. "Sugar Franklin is dead."

I walked into the living room and put the cage down in front of the bookcase beside the kitchen.

"I'm sorry," I told the birds. "Sugar Franklin died last night. She won't be coming back."

I kept having to remember to breathe. I felt as if I were on some kind of remote control, mechanically moving here and there, picking this up, putting that down.

I called the office and told our secretary I was ill and wouldn't be in. I could barely recognize my own voice. I opened my laptop and wrote a short note to my friends and to the Tiel Talk board, simply saying she'd died in the night.

I sat down on the couch and cried. I began to wonder just how much grief a person could endure before they, too, died late in the night.

After awhile Christine called to check on me. "I'm okay," I said.

I remembered again to breathe. "I should have kept her home," I said suddenly. "I should have let her die at home. I knew she wasn't egg bound."

"You did the right thing," Christine said.

I shook my head. No, I was quite certain I should have kept her at home, let her die where she was safe, not surrounded by strangers who kept poking her with things, not left alone all night in an incubator. Did she wonder where I was? Did she hate me for leaving her all alone in a dark strange place with strange noises? Why, why hadn't I kept her home? Had she chirped for me and received only silence in return?

I turned on the television and stared at it for a while.

An hour or so later the door bell rang. I cursed under my breath. It was probably some well-meaning friend but I couldn't deal with anyone right now. I just couldn't.

I opened the door and saw a woman standing there, smiling, with a huge bouquet of flowers. Probably wanting directions, I thought. No one ever sent me flowers.

"Ms. Floyd?" she said. She looked at my face and her smile faded.

I nodded. She offered me the flowers.

"Is it bad," she asked.

I nodded and took the flowers.

"I'm sorry," she said. "I hope it gets better soon." She took a step back and said, "Blessings upon you." I watched her get into her car and drive away.

The card said from Squawkers and friends." Daisies and baby's breath and roses. I put them on the table and began crying again.

Finally, I logged on and wrote to Bev and Christine, thanking them for the flowers.

I knew I had to deal with Sugar Franklin's cage as soon as possible, while I was still numb. I knew if I waited it would sit there for months, tormenting me with its emptiness.

The newspaper on the bottom of the cage had one very large stain and some remaining clear liquid in it. I hadn't noticed it the day before. Her kidneys, I remembered.

I unplugged the AviTemp and put it away. I took down each toy and unscrewed each perch. I put them in the trash because I couldn't bear to think of any other bird touching them.

None of the other birds fussed at me; they just watched.

I sprayed the cage with cleaner and wiped off the bars. It really needed a good scrubbing, but I didn't have the energy. I left it at that.

I went back on the Internet and pulled up the death jewelry site I'd studied so carefully so long ago. I ordered a cremation necklace. I decided I would bury her ashes by the bird feeder, just outside the glass patio doors. She always enjoyed watching things outside from her cage. I would find some small object as a marker so I would always be able to see it from the living room, know she was there.

I sent an e-mail to Christine.

"The box they bring back to the vet with the ashes, how big is it? The size of a shoebox? Smaller? There's a guy who's coming to mow the yard next week and I'm going to ask him to dig a deep hole so I won't have to do it. And do you think it would be okay to put a few grains of millet into a locket with some of her ashes? I mean, it won't rot or turn into maggots or something, will it? I don't plan to re-open it; in fact, I was thinking of maybe gluing it closed once I'd put the ashes in, but I'd hate for it to start smelling or something. Grief sucks."

Christine wrote back immediately. "The box will be very small. Like maybe a small index card file. Millet shouldn't cause a problem in your locket. The Egyptians put grain and such in with their loved ones. Also, I believe they usually recommend glue to seal it permanently. And yes, grief sucks."

I took a deep breath and logged into Tiel Talk.

From LC in South Africa, "Oh my word no! No! NO! I refuse to believe this! She was truly one amazing little tiel and will forever be sorely missed. Oh, my heart is so broken now, the tears streaming down my face and I can just imagine all the hurt you must be going through. Rest in peace, little Angel."

From AL in Canada: "I am weeping with you, dear friend. May your baby fly free and high and get into all kinds of trouble on the Rainbow Bridge...she had a good full life with you honey...she knew she was loved and that is for sure."

There were dozens more posts on Tiel Talk from well-meaning members, most of them strangers to me. I scrolled through the list and stopped when I came to this one:

"I'm sorry you lost her. She misses you, too."

I sat back and stared at the screen. "She misses you, too." She was dead, how could she miss me? Wasn't death the great peace bringer of all living things? How could she miss me? I closed my eyes and felt more tears roll down my face. Did she miss me? Was it possible? Perhaps her consciousness was still hovering around Pennyroyal or even here? Was she even now calling for me, wondering why I didn't answer?

I logged off the computer. I knew if I didn't pull myself together I would go mad.

Over the next few days I kept asking myself impossible questions -- why hadn't I kept her at home to die? Had she died in pain? Had she called for me and heard nothing but the train rumbling past the clinic? What could I have done differently? Did I do something I shouldn't have? The thought of her being in pain as she died began to haunt me, but there was no way to know and no one to ask. I knew whoever I talked to would be more concerned about my emotional state than about telling me the unvarnished truth of death mechanics.

I suddenly thought of Liz, who I had not talked with for a couple of years. She would not mince words, I realized. She would tell me the truth. I wrote her:

Dear Liz:

Sugar Franklin died Tuesday night, and I have the same question every pet owner wants to know -- did she suffer?

I'm asking you because I think you'll be straight with me and not sugarcoat, at least about this anyway.

Does the body produce some sort of narcotic that takes away pain as the systems shut down? Did she just fall into a nice final sleep, unaware? Or did she hurt so much inside that death was the only escape? Please don't sugarcoat it for me -- I have three other parrots that might require such drastic care at some point and I have to think of their well being, too.

Everyone has been wonderful to me through all this and I am very grateful for them; some of them even sent me yellow and white flowers -- the same color of Sugar Franklin's little feathers.

But did she suffer, Liz? Was there anything I could have done differently or anything I should have known but didn't or were there signs I should have seen but didn't? Did she suffer, Liz?

I don't know why it hadn't occurred to me before, but on the following Monday I called Dr. Lacki and asked her if Sugar Franklin had suffered before she died. After all, she was her veterinarian and would know.

No, she told me, she didn't think so. When she had arrived that morning the techs told her that there had been no signs of struggle or vomiting. She reminded me that Sugar Franklin was full of formula, medication, and fluids and inside a nice warm incubator; in other words, she had had everything she needed to improve if she had been able. I absolutely had done the right thing by bringing her into the clinic -- I could not provide the type of heat she needed at home or have been able to force fluids and meds down her throat.

That there had been no signs of struggle made me feel better.

I received an e-mail from Liz:

Dearest Marguerite –

Having known you as a bird owner and friend, I would say you did everything possible for Sugar Franklin. Indeed, you went far beyond what the "average" parrot owner would've gone. The fact that Dr. Z was gone when you needed her most was one of those horrid ironies that Life likes to toss in every once in a while, as you will no doubt wonder if she could've save Sugar if she'd been there. But you are realistic enough to know that Dr. Z might not've been able to save her either.

It is important for you to realize that the process of grieving includes guilt, whether you deserve to feel guilty or not. Like I used to tell veterinary clients, when you have a head cold, your nose runs. It is just part of the process. Your nose doesn't run because you *deserve* it or because you're a terrible person or because you are a failure at something. Your nose runs because that is a symptom of having a head cold.

It is the same with grief. When someone you love dies, you feel guilty – not because you deserve to or did anything wrong, but because that is a primary symptom of the grieving process. Men tend to turn that guilt outward and it manifests as anger – at the medical profession, what or whomever. We woman are oh, so prone to turning that anger inward and hurting ourselves with it. It's as if blaming yourself is better than accepting that there was nothing you could've done. Anything is worse than being helpless, after all.

Are they suffering at that stage? I don't think so. As the body is shutting down for any reason, it makes sense that it would not waste energy in acute nerve responses. After all, why would that body wish to do such a thing when it is dying? The function of pain is to warn the animal to avoid something so it can survive. When it is dying, it no longer needs such a response. So no, I do not think Sugar Franklin suffered, Marguerite.

As to whether or not you should've brought her home, again I don't think so. Having watched three humans and innumerable animals die, most are unconscious long before their hearts stop, and I don't think they are aware of who is around them.

But I do know that statistics say something rather poignant about humans. The death rate in human hospitals goes way up after visiting hours end . . . not because the quality of care drops. It is as if – and this is from a dear friend who was a hospice nurse for years – people wait until their loved ones are gone. We also know that animals tend to wander away to die. So death may very well be a private thing that is not to be shared . . . despite all the dramatic death scenes we've seen on TV and in movies.

I also know that if I'd been in your place with Sugar Franklin in such bad shape, and if I'd kept her home with me, I would've stayed up with her. I would've held her and stroked her and whispered to her . . . and she wouldn't have been able to even doze off with my constant loving attention. So it would be much more likely that she would've suffered more if I'd kept her with me.

Besides from what I have witnessed at various deathbeds, I do not think that would've been what Sugar Franklin would've wanted. *She needed you to let her go, as she loved you and leaving you wasn't easy. By leaving her in the warm and caring hands at the vet hospital, you gave her the freedom to leave whenever she was ready to do so.*

In other words, be at ease, Marguerite. Your grief is testimonial to what a great bird Sugar Franklin was and how much you loved her in the years you had together. You'll never stop missing her, but the pain will ease and so will the guilt.

Liz

Chapter Nineteen

For a few days after Sugar Franklin died, Nicholas
began giving alarm calls. He would crane his neck
and head toward Sugar's cage then look back at me. I
told him again that Sugar was dead and we couldn't
bring her back, and that I missed her, too. He did it
for several days, and I went through the explanation
each time. I held him and petted him, but he would
not be consoled.

One night before I covered the up the
cockatiels I noticed they'd thrown out all the little
wicker balls from their toy dish. I put them all back
and forgot about it. The next day, just as I was
getting ready to meet a friend for lunch, I glanced in
the cage -- and all the balls were out again. I didn't
remember ever seeing all of them out of the bowl
before the night before. As I stacked them up again,
it came to me that it was Sugar's doing. But wasn't it
too soon for her to be haunting the house?

A co-worker told me how her mom always
wanted a dog but never got one for one reason or
another. As her mother was dying, the friend asked
for a sign -- like a white bird. The day her mother
died, she and her siblings went to her mom's house
and there, at the back door, was a white dog with no
collar, scratching to get in. They'd never seen it
before or again. Was Sugar Franklin throwing out
the wicker balls to let me know she was all right?

The guy who mowed my yard dug a small
deep hole in the back yard for Sugar's ashes. After he
left I considered how cold and wet the ground was
and even when it warmed up later in the year it

would still be cold and miserable.

I thought about just holding her ashes in my palm and letting the wind take them. After all, she was a bird, a thing of wind and wings. But I felt that same old fear of her accidently flying away, getting lost or hurt. She didn't belong in the dirt. She belonged with me.

I went online and ordered a small container to put the rest of her ashes in.

I cleaned out the cart Sugar's cage sat on; threw out old broken things, cleaned off toys and perches and supplies and put them all in a huge plastic bag in the study closet.

Then I cleaned the cart and took it apart. The only thing left was to clean her cage itself. When that was done I put the cart and cage in the little storage building outside. Every time I glanced outside I saw the waiting open grave. No, I couldn't put her in such a cold and wet place. She needed to be home, safe and warm, with me.

All the birds watched this activity very carefully and quietly -- whether because they thought it concerned Sugar Franklin or because they couldn't remember the last time I actually cleaned anything, I don't know. Just in case, I explained it to them again.

When bedtimes came now, everyone went willingly -- no hissing or fighting or whining or "Look! I can hang upside down by one toe nail!" Maybe they were afraid I'd take them away the way I did Sugar and not bring them back either.

For such a small footprint in the living room there seemed to be a huge amount of open space where her cage was, physically. Maybe one day I could buy a recliner or a nice non-chew-up-able chair to put beside the couch. The empty space felt large enough to hold an entire other house.

In the evenings I was aware that it took a lot less time to get everyone fed and petted and fussed over. I didn't think I had routinely spent all that much more time with Sugar than the others but maybe I had.

When the ashes were ready, I picked them up after work. They were in a white box, maybe six inches square, with the crematorium's address and Sugar Franklin's name on it. On the drive home, I turned the car radio to the jazz station and caught myself telling her that we'd be home soon, just as I had so many times before, as if it was actually her sitting beside me.

Inside the box were the cremation certificate and a huge amount of white tissue paper. Under the tissue paper was a large clear plastic bag. When I freed the bag from the tissue paper there were the ashes inside. Much lighter in color than I had imagined they would be, and about the texture of very fine-grained sand. Maybe barely a tablespoon full. Such a tiny amount for such a huge life.

It wasn't as bad as I thought it would be. Somehow it was comforting to have her with me -- even though it was just a scant tablespoon of ashes. It took me a while to put some of the ashes in the pendent because the hole in the pendant was so tiny, but I did and then put it on. The pendant fell down my chest to just about the top of my heart, which was her second most favorite spot on my body, after my shoulder.

A week or so later my mom and I met for lunch and shopping, and when I got home there was a letter from Iowa State University. My first thought was that it might be a sympathy note from Dr. Z. I had already received a nice card from Pennyroyal, with little notes from everyone who knew her and cared for Sugar Franklin, which was so sweet and heartbreaking I had broken down in tears.

When I opened the envelope there was a glossy brochure in it, and I was prepared to think very bad things about Dr. Z if she was asking for institutional donations. But instead, the letter said that the Pennyroyal veterinarians had made a donation in Sugar Franklin's name to the Companion Animal Fund of the College of Veterinary Medicine. The glossy brochure was about the fund.

The letter ended with, "We hope you will take comfort from knowing that, despite your loss, you have had the privilege, responsibility, and joy as a keeper of one of God's creatures."

Which made me cry all over again because Sugar Franklin was a privilege, a responsibility, and my joy.

Afterword

It was several years before I could speak of Sugar Franklin without tears. My parrot friends encouraged me to talk about Sugar Franklin and always offered as much sympathy and caring as I might need. I was grateful that I no longer had the type of friends who would tell me to cheer up and just go get another bird. There is no replacement for Sugar Franklin.

One of the songs for the women's chorus the semester she died was "My Funny Valentine." While the first sopranos sang the melody and us second sopranos waited to provide harmony, I would sing to myself a revised version.

"My little yellow bird,
Sweet comic yellow bird.
You make me smile with my heart."

and

"Don't change a hair for me,
Not if you care for me.
Stay, little yellow bird, stay."

I still sometimes wear the locket with her ashes in it. I still occasionally forget and get out one too many food dishes or treat sticks, as if she were still here, pacing back and forth, back and forth, to either be let out or given Nutriberries. I still hurt when I realize my mistake.

Patches continues to thrive under LC's care. She is still afraid of hands, but her leg healed completely and she is totally feathered. There is no physical trace of the abuse and damage she suffered.

LC wrote that "She calls to me from her cage, and answers me back when I talk to her. She gets happy when she sees me after I have been out for the morning. This little baby the vets gave up for dead is truly a miracle baby."

LC began rescuing other birds and now her South African home is full of rescued parrots and songbirds.

One of Bev's and Marty's cockatiels died suddenly, and they rescued another; both are healthy and suitably adored. Sometimes Bev and I go out to Most Valuable Pets to play with the macaws and cockatoos and amazons, and to remind each other not to buy another parrot no matter how cute it is.

Christine still has George, who continues to dote on her above all other members of the family. She has added a tiny, bossy green-cheek conure named Lulu to her household. George and Lulu insist on helping Christine when she is trying to knit socks.

My remaining three parrots are all healthy and happy and spoiled. Nicholas and Flash share a large cage and continue their big brother-little brother relationship, with occasional squabbles to clarify ever-changing territorial issues. Charli still spends most of her time upside down and attempting to chew all the books in the house. I post silly pictures and stories about them on Facebook the way all besotted parrot lovers do.

They missed Sugar Franklin for a long time. About a year after her death I needed to move her little travel cage from in front of the bookcase where I had put it when she died. I was shocked when the cockatiels and Charli began shrieking and yelling at me until I put it down again. There is no question in my mind that they knew it was her cage, even after such a long absence.

Once in a while I will play small videos I took of Sugar Franklin. The cockatiels will give out their contact calls when they hear her voice. They do not give contact calls when hearing any other cockatiel over the Internet.

I took early retirement from my job and began teaching online for another university. I was able to begin seriously writing again and even wrote a small book about the African brown-headed parrot.

People continue to try to give me rescued parrots, and I continue to refuse. My first responsibility is to Charli, Flash, and Nicholas; taking on another parrot would necessarily take from them some of the love, care, and time I've already promised.

My mother has given up on any of my parrots talking, but she loves hearing Nicholas give her the wolf whistle when she visits.

My life improves every day in so many ways, and I am grateful for all I have.

But I rarely listen to jazz any more.